Hussein Abdul-Raof

Arabic Stylistics

Hussein Abdul-Raof

Arabic Stylistics
A Coursebook

2001
Harrassowitz Verlag · Wiesbaden

Die Deutsche Bibliothek – CIP-Einheitsaufnahme
Ein Titeldatensatz für diese Publikation ist bei Der Deutschen Bibliothek erhältlich

Die Deutsche Bibliothek – CIP Cataloguing-in-Publication-Data
A catalogue record for this publication is available from Die Deutsche Bibliothek

e-mail: cip@dbf.ddb.de

Printed on permanent/durable paper.
Typesetting by Abdassamad Clarke, Charlottenlund, Denmark
Printing and binding by KN Digital Printforce GmbH, Stuttgart
Printed in Germany

ISBN 3-447-04435-7

For

learners and teachers of Arabic

الإهداء

إلى عُشَّاقِ العربيَّةِ وأساتِذَتِها

Contents

Acknowledgements

It is a great pleasure to record my warmest thanks to Dr Partick Leach, former lecturer in linguistics at the Department of Linguistics and Phonetics, University of Leeds, for the generous time he gave me to discuss and read the manuscript of this book. I also wish to thank Professor Yasir Suleiman, Department of Islamic and Middle Eastern Studies, University of Edinburgh, Professor Clive Holes, Oriental Institute, Oxford University, Dr Dionisius Agius, Department of Arabic and Middle Eastern Studies, University of Leeds, Mr Lee Davidson, Department of Linguistics and Phonetics, University of Leeds, Dr Peter Howarth, the Language Centre, Univeristy of Leeds, and Dr James Dickins, Centre for Middle Eastern and Islamic Studies, University of Durham, for their time to discuss with me my research plan. I am also grateful to Dr Said Faiq, School of Languages, University of Salford, for his advice and comments.

Abbreviations

f	feminine
fpl	feminine plural
fs	feminine singular
m	masculine
mpl	masculine plural
ms	masculine singular

Introduction

The main purpose of this book is systematically to develop, promote and upgrade the writing skills of learners of Arabic as a foreign language through an in-depth analysis of the stylistic aspects of modern standard Arabic. I felt, through my teaching of Arabic and Arabic stylistics, the urgent need among students for such a book that enables the learner to acquire stylistic competence in a gradual and exemplified manner where the theoretical notions are supported by generous examples.

I have realized from experience that intermediate level students have acquired some knowledge of grammar, learned some vocabulary, developed basic communicative skills, and are able to read Arabic. They also need, at this stage, a book that explains to them the stylistic mechanism of Arabic, on the one hand, and illustrates for them what and how they can produce stylistically sound and effective Arabic, on the other. Without a thorough understanding of the stylistic and linguistic mechanism involved in the production of effective Arabic, awareness of the recurrent structural patterns, and familiarity with the subtle linguistic interaction of words intra- and inter-sententially, the student's linguistic competence in producing effective Arabic cannot be achieved. Learning Arabic stylistics is, therefore, a necessary skill for all learners of Arabic as a foreign language. This book also aims to develop students' analytical stylistic and linguistic insight needed for their next advanced or postgraduate stage. This book, however, is not intended to be a book on Arabic grammar or linguistics.

There isn't, however, any book available on Arabic stylistics for students to consult although Arabic as a foreign language is taught all over the world and the need among students for knowing how Arabic writing works is evident. The teachers of Arabic as a foreign language also need this kind of book to assist them in developing their students' practical ability and understanding of Arabic.

This book includes six chapters presented coherently in the light of the main objective of studying stylistics. Chapter One lays the grammatical foundation and presents to the student the most recurrent structural patterns in Arabic which he/she encounters and needs to produce. It provides 61 possible structures which can be learned, reproduced in writing, or employed in a practical stylistic linguistic analysis. The student is made aware of the major stylistic distinction in Arabic between basic and derived sentence structures. Basic sentence structure is subclassified into transitive/intransitive sentence structure and equative sentence structure. Other possible structures which can branch off the basic and derived structures are also provided. Each of the 61 patterns is supported by a variety of examples. Chapter One, therefore, sets the linguistic scene for the student. Chapter Two discusses in detail the building blocks, i.e., words, that occur in the different structures presented in Chapter One. Chapter Two provides a thorough description of Arabic lexical items; it starts off with a classification of vocabulary and moves on to provide an account of key semantic notions such as semantic fields, collocation, collocational restrictions, connotation, ameliorative and pejorative expressions, emotiveness, colligation, synonyms, antonyms, hyponyms, polysemes, homonyms, acronyms; other important lexical notions are also discussed such as word set, idioms, courtesy and proverbial expressions, modes of address, calques and loan words. Examples are provided to support the understanding of each notion.

After laying the bricks needed in the construction of various structures, the student needs to be familiar with what makes these words and sentences hang together. In other words, it is essential for students to understand the cohesion network in Arabic and be familiar with the subtle and crucial textural interrelations between words and sentences in an extended text of more than one sentence. For this purpose, in Chapter Three, Arabic text structure and the major types of cohesion - reference, substitution, ellipsis, conjunction, and lexical cohesion - are thoroughly discussed with illuminating examples. These cohesive elements enable the student to understand the intra- and inter-sentential cohesive relations without which the text does not cohere and falls apart.

After we have introduced the cohesion mechanism at sentence and text level, Chapter Four introduces the student to the major text types in Arabic together with the characteristic hallmarks of each text type. A wide variety of authentic texts are used as examples to familiarize the student with actual modern standard Arabic. In Chapter Five, the student is introduced to the decorative aspect of Arabic; at this stage, the student is expected to have built up a sound stylistic linguistic foundation. The introduction of the rhetorical aspects of Arabic in Chapter Five is intended to enhance the student's stylistic competence and enable him/her produce more effective and elaborate Arabic. The list of 25 figures of speech is also of great value to the stylistic analysis of Arabic texts. Each figure of speech is supported by examples most of which are authentic and taken from a variety of sources. Chapter Six is intended to put the five chapters into practice. It provides a checklist of grammatical, lexical, cohesive, textual, and rhetorical features. This chapter tests the student's practical ability to undertake an in-depth stylistic analysis of authentic Arabic texts. It is a kind of a summary of the five chapters and is a very useful practical exercise for the student.

Examples, Translations and Exercises

In order to develop and upgrade the student's practical ability in both writing and stylistic analysis, generous examples are provided throughout the book. Most of these examples are taken from a wide variety of authentic sources to mirror the actual Arabic in use which students need to practise in real working life. These examples are provided with translations which are intended to help the student to understand the examples and their relevant notions. It is important to note that some of the translations cannot achieve total equivalence to the actual meaning expressed by the Arabic example. This applies to examples of some derived structures, thematic organization, connotation, denotation, emotive expressions, some modes of address, and rhetorical expressions. This is due to the fact that Arabic and English are linguistically and culturally incongruous languages. As culture is part and parcel of language, the approach of literal translation has been adopted in the translation of some Arabic texts such as letters in order to preserve the emotive and cultural flavour of Arabic. We have also avoided the use of vocalization in our examples as modern written Arabic does not use it. The student needs to supply his/her vocalization according to the grammatical context. The examples at the end of each chapter are very useful for the comprehension of the chapter and for classroom activities. They can be given as homework and discussed later on. Some of the sources of the texts provided in the practical exercises are not given in order to save space for more important discussion.

Chapter One
Sentence Structure
تركيب الجُملة العربية

1. 1 Introduction

If we look at a continuous Arabic text, we will see that most written sentences (delimited by a full stop, question mark or exclamation mark) contain at least one main clause. The few that do not are considered as minor sentences (see 1.2.11 and 1.2.12). The main clause(s) will indicate the function of the sentence, i.e., whether it is a statement (a declarative sentence), a question (an interrogative one) or an order (an imperative). A sentence containing just one main clause will be called a simple sentence. Basic clauses (hence simple sentences) can be affirmative or negative, and active or passive in form and are made up of a number of major constituents which may be verbal (a lexical verb, with or without accompanying auxiliaries and verbal particles), nominal (a noun, with or without adjective(s) or other modifiers, or a pronoun), or prepositional (a preposition + a nominal). These constituents have functions relating one with the other, such as Subject (a nominal), Verb (a verbal), Object (a nominal), Complement (a nominal) an Adjunct (a prepositional or nominal expression). The constituents in main clauses/simple sentences occur in various orders, according to the demands of the text. Subordinate clauses are more rigid in their ordering. To give an account of clause constituents and their ordering, we shall consider declarative, affirmative, active simple sentences, quoted out of any context, as basic, and other sentences as derived.

1.2 Basic Declarative Sentence Structure تركيب الجُملة الخبرية البسيطة

We can take simple affirmative active declarative sentences as basic. From them, we can derive, by simple rules, all sorts of other sentences (setting aside the minor sentence types mentioned in section 1.2.11 and 1.2.12). All these sentences will have, actually or implicitly, at least two constituents, a Subject and a Verb; some will have, in addition, further constituents, depending on the verb-type, as exemplified below.

1.2.1 Transitive/Intransitive Sentence Structure تركيبُ الجُملة بفعلٍ لازمٍ/مُتعد

The basic declarative sentence structure in Arabic is that which begins with a main verb. It is the unmarked linguistic pattern which is prototypically characterized by a high frequency of occurrence and usage. Arabic shows a stronger preference for the verb-initial pattern over other linguistic non-basic patterns. The prototypical basic sentence structures in Arabic are represented by the following patterns:

1. Verb + Subject

إنفتحت الباب – The door opened.

نام الرجل – The man slept.

جاءت الطبيبة – The doctor has come.

ضعفت وحدتهم – Their unity weakened.

2. Verb + Subject + Object

فحص الطبيب المريض - The doctor examined the patient.

سوف تنشر الصحف الخبر – The newspapers will publish the news.

أضعفت الخلافات وحدتهم – Disagreements weakened their unity.

أخلف صديقي وعده – My friend broke his promise.

أنتظر ردّكم – I expect your reply.

أتوقّع موافقتكم – I expect your approval.

3. Verb + Subject + Prepositional Object

يبحث سالم عن بيت للايجار – Salim is looking for a house to rent.

فكرت بمقترح جديد – I thought of a new proposal.

أتطلع الى لقائكم – I look forward to seeing you.

رحب حارث بنا – Harith welcomed us.

4. Verb + Subject + Adjunct

جلس سالم جلسة غريبة - Salim sat in a strange way.

نامت سعاد نوما عميقا - Suad slept fast.

إنخفضت الأسعار إنخفاضا حادا - Prices dropped sharply.

فاز فوزا ساحقا - He won a landslide victory.

إنفتحت الباب بقوة - The door opened violently.

مات الرجل فجأة - The man died suddenly.

جاءت الطبيبة مسرعة - The doctor came in a hurry.

وقع الرجل الاعمى في الحفرة - The blind man fell in the ditch.

5. Verb + Subject+ Object + Adjunct

فحص الطبيب المريض فحصا دقيقا - The doctor examined the patient thoroughly.

نام الطفل نوما عميقا - The baby slept fast.
ضرب الشرطي اللص ضربا مبرحا - The policeman hit the thief hard.
سأتصل بك بعد وصولي - I shall contact you immediately after I arrive.
سأخبركم قبل ذهابى - I shall inform you before I go.
سأخبركم بعد الظهر - I will inform you after lunch.
كلّمتني قبل منتصف الليل - She talked to me before midnight.
ستلتقي هدى بالوفد بعد قليل - Huda will meet the delegation in a moment.
كتب مروان الرسالة في الحديقة - Marwan wrote the letter in the garden.
وقّع سالم العقد في لندن - Salim signed the contract in London.

6. Verb + Subject+ Indirect Object + Direct Object
أعطت عائشة المدير الكتاب - Aysha gave the headmaster the book.
وصف الطبيب المريض دواء - The doctor prescribed the patient medicine.

7. Verb + Subject+ Direct Object + Preposition + Indirect Object
ستعطي عائشة الكتاب إلى المدير - Aysha will give the book to the headmaster.
وصف الطبيب دواء إلى المريض - The doctor prescribed medicine to the patient.

8. Verb + Subject + Object + Object Complement
نصّب زيد سالماً وزيراً - Zaid appointed Salim a minister.
إنتخب زيد سالماً رئيساً - Zaid elected Salim president.
جعل زيد سالماً سعيداً - Zaid made Salim happy.

It is important to note that the auxiliary verb (كان - used to, was/were) can occur before the verb in all the above structures, as in:

كان يكتب زيد الرسالة عندما دق الهاتف - Zaid was writing the letter when the telephone rang.
كنا نسبح في نهر دجلة في العطلة الصيفية - We used to swim in the Tigris during the summer holidays.
كانت لا تنام حتى تنهي جميع واجباتها - She did not use to go to bed before she had finished all her work.

Other aspectual verbs like (بدأ ، أخذ ، مازال) and verbal particles like (لن لم ، قد ، سوف ، سـ) can also occur before the verb in all the above structures, as in:

مازالت تأكل عندما دخل هشام - She was still eating when Hisham came in.
أخذ الطفل يبكي عند وصول الطبيب - The baby started crying once the doctor arrived.
قد لاتنام حتى تنهي واجباتها - She may not go to sleep until she finishes her work.

In a decontextualized situation, i.e., when the sentence occurs on its own, the main verb-initial structure implies that the subject occurs first in the absence of a morphological disambiguating element, as in:

قتل موسى يحيى

which, as it stands, can only mean (Musa killed Yahya) since both nouns end with a final weak radical (i.e., indeclinable final vowel) (حـــرف ناقـص) which cannot take the nominative (الرفـع) or the accusative (النـصب) case marking that can disambiguate the meaning.

We also need to note that adjuncts (sometimes called adverbials) in Arabic are mobile and can appear at different places in the sentence. Thus, we can find Subject-final sentences, as in:

وصل الى لندن يوم أمس الرئيس السوفيتي الجديد - The new Russian president arrived in London yesterday.

غادر الى واشنطن صباح هذا اليوم الرئيس المصري - The Egyptian president left for Washington this morning.

The Subjects are (الرئيس السوفيتي الجديد) and (الرئيس المصري).

1.2.2 Equative Sentence Structure الجُملة البسيطة بلا فعل رئيسي

These are sentences without a main lexical verb. These can be sub-classified into three main categories:

(i) equative sentence structures without any lexical verb

These are represented by the linguistic pattern:

9. Subject + Subject Complement

الحق واضح - Truth is evident.

العلم نافع - Knowledge is useful.

الجو لطيف - The weather is nice.

أنتَ على حق - You are right.

أحمد صحفي - Ahmad is a journalist.

وسائل الإعلام صامتة - The media is silent.

محمد عريق النسب - Muhammad is highborn.

عائشة أم المؤمنين - Aysha is the mother of believers.

رئيس القسم رجل عبقري - The head of department is a genius.

(ii) equative sentence structures with one of the (كان) set

Arabic sentence structures of this category contain one of the (كان) set of auxiliary verbs (كان وأخواتها) which are (صار ، أصبح ، أمسى ، بات ، بقي ، مادام ، ليس ، ما عاد ، ما زال); this type of sentence structure is represented by the following linguistic pattern:

10. One of the (كان) *Auxiliary Set + Subject + Subject Complement*
كان الحق واضحاً - The truth was evident.
كان الجو لطيفاً - The weather was nice.
مادام سالم فقيراً - Salim is still a poor man.
ليس الفقر عيباً - Poverty is not a shame.
صار الوضع متوتراً - The situation has become tense.
أصبح السلام مستحيلاً - Peace has become impossible.
(iii) equative sentence structures with a sentence-initial particle (أنّ/إنّ)
This category of Arabic sentence structures contain one of the (إنّ/أنّ) set of auxiliary verbs (انّ وأخواتها) which are (لكنّ ، كأنّ ، ليت ، لعلّ); the following linguistic pattern represents this kind of linguistic pattern:
11. One of the (أنّ/إنّ) *Auxiliary Set + Subject + Subject Complement*
إنّ الجوَّ لطيفٌ - Verily, the weather is nice.
كأنّ الدرسَ مُمتعٌ - The lesson seems to be interesting.

1.2.3 Imperative Structure جُملة الأمر

Note that all basic structures can appear as imperatives whether affirmatives or negatives, as in 12 and 13:

12. Imperative Verb + رجاءاً
إجلسوا رجاءاً - Sit down, please !
إنتبه رجاءاً - Listen, please !
ضع الطعام على الطاولة - Put the food on the table.
قف - Stop !
إخرس - Shut up !
إسكت - Be quiet !
قُل الحق - Say the truth !

The imperative with the auxiliary (كانَ) takes the pattern:
13. Imperative كُنْ *+ Subject Complement*
كن صادقاً - Be truthful!
كن صبورا - Be patient!
كوني مخلصة - Be faithful!
كونوا مجدّين - Be hard working!

It is important to note that imperatives can, of course, have any of the objects or adjuncts listed in our basic sentences and can also be negative (see below).

1.2.4 Negative Structure جُملة النفي

(i) negative declaratives

14. لا / سوفَ لا / ما / لن / سوفَ لن / لم *+ Sentence*

لا أحب اللحوم - I do not like meat.

سوف لا أحضر الإجتماع - I shall not go to the meeting.

ما أريد أن أذهب - I do not want to go.

ما زيد بغني - Zaid is not rich.

ما أنا بكاذب - I am not a liar.

لن أقبل بذلك - I do not accept that.

سوف لن تتكلم معهم - She will not speak with them.

لم أكمل كلامي - I have not finished my statement.

لاتكن صبوراً - Do not be patient!

لاتكن منافقاً - Do not be a hypocrite!

لاتقل الحق - Do not say the truth!

(ii) basic structures with copulative verbs

15. لَيْسَ *+ Subject + Subject Complement*

or:

Subject + لَيْسَ *+ Subject Complement*

ليس الجواب واضحاً - The answer is not clear.

الجواب ليس واضحاً - The answer is not clear.

أنا لست كاذباً - I am not a liar.

أليس الجواب واضحاً - Isn't the answer clear?

1.2.5 Imperative Negative Structure جُملة الأمر المنفي

16. لا *+ Verb*

لا تبذر أموالك - Do not waste your money !

لا تستغل أصدقائك - Do not take advantage of your friends !

لا تكذب - Do not lie !

1.2.6 Interrogative Verbal Structure الجُملة الفعلية الإستفهامية

17. كَم / هَل / مَنْ / اينَ / لماذا . . . إلخ *+ Verb + Object/Subject*

من فتح الباب؟ - Who opened the door?

لماذا تأخرت؟ - Why are you late?

هل سافر الرجل؟ - Has the man travelled?

Interrogative structures can also be formed by prefixing the interrogative bound morpheme (أ) i.e. (همزة الإستفهام) before the noun, as in:

أزيدٌ سافر؟ - Was it Zaid who travelled?

or before the pronoun, as in:

أأنتَ كتبتَ هذا؟ - Was it you who wrote this?

or before the verb, as in:

أتُسافرين اليوم؟ - Are you going to travel today?

Interrogatives can also be negative and passive, as in:

ألم أقُل لكَ ذلك ؟ - Didn't I tell you that?

ألم يسافر زيد ؟ - Didn't Zaid travel?

لماذا يُضطهد الشعب ؟ - Why are people oppressed?

1.2.7 Exception Structure جُملة الإستثناء

18. ما + *Verb* + أحد + إلاَّ / غيرَ + *Subject*

ما نجح أحد غير أحلام - No one passed except Ahlam.

ما بقي أحد إلا إبراهيم - No one stayed except Ibrahim.

19. ما + *Verb* + *Subject* + *Object* + إلاَّ / غيرَ + *Object Complement*

ما أكل زيد شيئاً إلا قطعة خبز - Zaid did not eat anything except a piece of bread.

ما قال عمر شيئاً غير الحق - Omar did not say anything but the truth.

Note that the object (شيئاً - anything) is not mentioned as it is implicitly understood. Thus we get sentences like:

ما أكل زيد إلا قطعة خبز - Zaid did not eat anything except a piece of bread.

ما قال عمر غير الحق - Omar did not say anything but the truth.

20. ما + *Verb* + أحد + *Object* + إلاَّ / غيرَ + *Subject*

ما تكلم أحد معي إلا أحلام - No one spoke to me except Ahlam.

ما تبرع أحد شيئاً غير أحمد - No one donated anything except Ahmad.

We may also find:

ما كلمني أحد غير أحلام - No one spoke to me except Ahlam,

where the direct object pronoun (ني - me) is cliticized on to the verb (كلم - spoke to).

21. Verb + *Subject* + ما خَلا / ما عَدا + *Subject*

نجح الطلاب ما عدا خالد - All students passed except Khalid.

وافق الجميع ما خلا طارق - Every one agreed except Tarik.

We have treated (خالد) and (طارق) as subjects because the underlying meaning is that (Khalid did not succeed) and (Tarik did not agree).

1.2.8 Passive Structure جُملة المبني للمجهول

22. Passive Verb + Subject

أُغلقت المدارس والجامعات - Schools and universities were closed.

قُصفت الأحياء المدنية بالمدفعية - The civilian quarters were shelled.

Of course, passive sentences can be negative and/or interrogative as well, as in:

لم تُغلق المدارس والجامعات - Schools and universities were not closed.

هل قُصِفت الأحياءُ المدنية بالمدفعية ؟ - Were the civilian quarters shelled?

1.2.9 Periphrastic Passive Structure جُملة المبني للمجهول المُسهبة

This is realized either by:

23. تم *+ Nominalization + Object*

تم إغلاق المدارس والجامعات - Schools and universities were closed.

تم تدمير المنشآت الحيوية - The infrastructure was destroyed.

or by: قام بـ . . . + Nominalization

24. قام *+ Subject +* بـ *+ Nominalization + Object*

قامت الشرطة باعتقال المُشتبه بهم - The police arrested the suspects.

قامت أجهزة الإعلام بشن حملة ضد هذا المشروع - The media launched a campaign against this plan.

The Past Participle can also be employed to denote the same meaning as that expressed by a passive or a periphrastic passive structure, as in:

المدارس والجامعات المُغلقة - the closed schools and universities

المنشآت الحيوية المُدمرة - the destroyed infrastructure

القصة المُبسطة - the simplified story

المُشتبه به - the suspect

1.2.10 Comparative Structure جُملة المُقارنة

25. Subject + أفضَلُ مِنْ / خَيرٌ مِنْ / أصغر من . . إلخ *+ Prepositional Phrase*

الصلاة خير من النوم - Prayers are more important than sleeping.

السباحة أفضل من الركض - Swimming is better than running.

هذا أصغر حجماً من ذلك - This is smaller than that.

التطعيم أقل ألماً من الحقنة - Vaccination is less painful than an injection.

عثمان أكثر حياءاً من غيره - Uthman is more shy than others.

1.2.11 Vocative Structure جُملة المُنادى

26. يا *+ Subject*
يا حامدة - O Hamidah !
يا أبا بكرٍ - O Abu Bakr !
يا عبد الله - O Abdullah !
يا رجلُ - O man !
يا هشامُ - O Hisham !
or يا أيُّها / ياايَّتُها *+ (definite) Subject*
يا أيها الرجلُ - O man !
يا أيتها البنتُ - O girl !
or without the vocative article (يا)*:*
أيها الرجلُ ، إيتها البنتُ

1.2.12 Public Sign Structure جُملة الإشارات العامة

27. Nominalization/Noun Phrase + Passive Participle/Interjection
التدخين ممنوع - No Smoking
الدخول ممنوع - No Entry
الهدوء رجاءاً - Quiet Please
الكلاب ممنوعة - No Dogs

28. Imperative Masculine Singular Verb
قف - Stop!
إنتَبه - Watch out!

29. Noun Phrase
ضغط عال - High Voltage!
خطر - Danger!
غرفة إنتظار - Waiting Room

30. Noun Phrase + Adjunct (or Prepositional Phrase)
نقطة تفتيش أمامك - Check Point Ahead!
شاحنات فقط - Trucks Only!
بيت للإيجار - House for Rent
سيارة للبيع - Car for Sale

1.3 Compound Structure الجُملة المُركَّبة

Types of co-ordination:
(i) Compound Noun Phrases

31. Verb + Compound Subject
جاء طارق وحامد - Tarik and Hamid came.
إحتج العمال والفلاحون - Workers and farmers made a protest.
or:

32. Verb + Subject + Compound Object
ساعد الشرطي أحمد وسالم - The policeman helped Ahmad and Salim.
أكلت التفاحة والبرتقالة - I ate the apple and the orange.
or:

33. Verb + Subject + Compound Adjective
بقيت سميرة صامتة ومستاءة - Samira remained silent and resentful.
ظل الوضع متوتراً ومتفجراً - The situation remained tense and explosive.

34. Compound Subject + Subject Complement
المدارس والمستشفيات ضرورية - Schools and hospitals are vital.
المناقشة والتمارين مفيدة - Discussion and exercises are useful.

(ii) Compound Adjuncts

35. Verb + Subject + Compound Adjunct
نلعب في المدرسة وفي المنتزه - We play at school and in the park.
ذهبت سلمى الى المكتبة والى السوق - Salma went to the library and to the market.

(iii) Compound Sentences

36. First Sentence + فـ / ثُمَّ / و + Second Sentence
قرأت الفصل وفهمته - I read the chapter and understood it.
قفز فكسر رجله - He jumped and broke his leg.
دخلت ثم جلست - She came in and sat down.

(iv) Compound Adjuncts

37. Verb + Subject + Compound Adjunct
يسوق زهير بسرعة وبطيش - Zuhair drives fast and without concentration.
تكلم منير بهدوء وبثقة - Munir talked calmly and with confidence.

(v) Interrogative Compound Sentences

38. Interrogative particle + Sentence + أو / أم + Sentence
هل سأل عني أحد أو ترك لي شيئاً؟ - Has anybody asked about me or left me something?
هل استلمت رسالة أم اتصل بكَ أحد؟ - Have you received a letter or has anyone contacted you?

(vi) Compound Sentences with Contrastive Conjuncts

39. Sentence + و لكنْ *+ Sentence*

أعرفه ولكن لا أعرف محل سكنه - I know him but I do not know where he lives.

هو مريض ولكن يفضل أن يمتحنَ - He is ill but he prefers to sit the exam.

(vii) Compound Sentences with Additive Conjuncts

40. ما / لا *+ Sentence +* ولا *+ Sentence*

ما تلوثت شفتاك بالحكمة ولا نضح لسانك بالفلسفة - Your lips were neither soiled by wisdom nor your tongue oozed philosophy.

لا يُسلِّم جاري على أحد ولا يتكلم مع أحد - My neighbour neither says hello to anyone nor speaks to anyone.

1.4 Derived Sentence Structure هيكل الجُملة المُشتقَّة

Although Arabic strongly favours the basic verb-initial word order, we also encounter the non-basic structure which starts with any other sentence constituent other than the lexical verb and its auxiliaries and particles. We can derive from the same basic verb-initial structure many other structures. These are the marked linguistic patterns which demonstrate a relatively free order of sentence constituents. The patterns which represent the derived sentence structures and the fluidity of word order in Arabic are:

41. Subject + Verb

المدرس وصل - The teacher arrived.

وحدتهم ضعفت - Their unity weakened.

42. Subject + Verb + Object

الإقتتال أضعف وحدتهم - Infighting weakened their unity.

الإعصار دمر المدينة - The hurricane destroyed the city.

الفضائح أفشلت حزب المحافظين - Scandals made the Conservative party fail.

43. Subject + Verb + Adjunct

الطلاب جلسوا في قاعة الامتحان - The students sat in the exam hall.

أنا أسافر غداً - I travel tomorrow.

حزب المحافظين فشل في الإنتخابات - The Conservative party failed in the elections.

الرجل الاعمى وقع في الحفرة - The blind man fell in the ditch.

البنت تدرس صباحاً - The girl studies in the morning.

44. Subject+ Verb + Object+ Adjunct

الأطفال يحبون اللعب في المنتزه - Children like playing in the park.

البنت إصطادت سمكة من البحيرة - The girl got a fish from the lake.

45. Subject + Verb + Indirect Object + Direct Object

عائشة أعطت المدير الكتاب - Aysha gave the headmaster the book.

رئيس الوزراء أعطى الشعب وعداً - The Prime Minister gave people a promise.

46. Subject + Verb + Direct Object+ Preposition + Indirect Object

عائشة أعطت الكتاب إلى المدير - Aysha gave the book to the headmaster.

رئيس الوزراء أعطى وعداً للشعب - The Prime Minister gave a promise to people.

Arabic also displays another set of derived structures which are prototypically characterized by an initial noun phrase that is in the nominative case (إسم مرفوع) but it is not the subject. This initial noun phrase in sentences (47-50) is called the theme (المُحدَّث عنه) (see 3.4 Thematic Structure); the subject of this type of derived structures agrees with the verb in number, person and gender, as in:

47. Object + Verb + Object Pronoun + Subject

المحسنُ يحبه الناس - As for the benevolent, people like him.

المُدرسةُ تزوجها أحمد - As for the (female) teacher, Ahmad married her.

البلدانُ النامية ندعمها نحن - As for the developing countries, we support them.

48. Object + Subject + Verb + Object Pronoun

المحسنُ الناسُ يحبونه - As for the benevolent person, the people like him.

المُدرسةُ أحمد تزوجها - As for the (female) teacher, Ahmad married her.

العقدُ أنتِ وقعتيه - As for the contract, you signed it.

49. Initial Noun Phrase + Verb + Subject + Possessive Pronoun (referring to initial noun phrase)

سالمٌ وصلت زوجته - As for Salim, his wife arrived.

الإعصارُ بقيت آثاره - As for the hurricane, its effect remained.

عمرُ فاز أبوه - As for Omar, his father won.

50. Initial Noun Phrase + Subject + Possessive Pronoun (referring to initial noun phrase) + Verb

سالمٌ زوجتُهُ وصلت - As for Salim, his wife arrived.

الإعصارُ آثاره بقيت - As for the hurricane, its effect remained.

عمرُ أبوه فاز - As for Omar, his father won.

Note that the fronted (initial) noun phrases in structures 47-50 are also in the nominative case and that an anaphoric pronoun (ضمير رابط) cliticized onto the verb (as in structures 47 and 48) or the noun (as in structures 49 and 50) is required. This anaphora refers to the fronted noun phrase. This is in contrast with the fronted noun phrases in structures 41-46 above.

Also note that the auxiliary (كان - used to, was/were) or (إنّ - verily) can be employed in all the above structures, as in:

كان الأطفال يلعبون في المنتزه - The children used to play (were playing) in the park.
إنّ الأطفال يلعبون في المنتزه - The children are playing in the park.

With the above derived structures, we can also have sentences whose structure is like (52):

51. إنّ *+ Subject +* قد *+ Transitive/Intransitive Verb*

or:

كان *+ Subject +* قد *+ Transitive/Intransitive Verb*

or :

لقد كان / وقد كان *+ Subject + Transitive/Intransitive Verb*

إنّ المدرس قد وصل - The teacher has arrived.
كان المدرس قد وصل - The teacher arrived.
وقد كان المدرس يصل كل يوم مبكراً - The teacher used to arrive every day early.
لقد كانت الخلافات التافهة تفتّت شملهم - Minor differences used to disintegrate their unity.
إنّ الفضائح قد أفشلت حزب المحافظين - Scandals verily made the Conservative party fail.
كانت البنت قد درست جميع الفصول - The girl had studied all the chapters.
كان رئيس الوزراء قد أعطى وعوداً للشعب - The Prime Minister gave promises to people.
وكانت واشنطن قد نفت إسقاط طائرة ركاب إيرانية - Washington denied the shooting down of an Iranian airbus.
لقد كان رئيس الوزراء يعطي وعوداً للشعب - The Prime Minister used to give promises to people.
إنّ المحسن قد يحبه الناس - As for the benevolent, people certainly like him.
وقد كان سالم تحبه زوجته كثيراً - As for Salim, his wife used to love him a lot.

Note that with (كان . . . قد) the verb is in the past tense but with (لقد . . . كان / وقد كان) the verb is in the present tense. With (إنّ . . . قد) the verb can be in the past or present tense. However, when the present tense verb is used with (إنّ . . . قد) the meaning of (قد) corresponds to (may) in English, as in:

إنّ المدرس قد يصل مبكراً - The teacher may arrive early.

Note that we can also encounter subject-final sentences, as in pattern 49:

52. كان في *+ Nominalization + Object + Subject*

وكان في استقبال السفير البريطاني الجديد وزير الخارجية الليبي - The new British ambassador was received by the Libyan minister for foreign affairs.

53. Subject + هو / هي / هم . . الخ *+ Relative Pronoun + Verb + Object*

حارث هو الذي كسر الشباك - It was Harith who broke the window.

الأطفال هم الذين يحبون هذا البرنامج - It is the children who love this programme.

التمارين هي التي تنفع الطلاب - It is the exercises which benefit the students.

54. أمّا *+ Subject +* فـ *+ Verb + Object*

أما أنا فأفضل الخضروات - As for me, I prefer vegetables.

أما الإتفاقية فسوف نوقعها قريباً - As for the agreement, we shall sign it soon.

أما الفصل الثاني فقد شرحته مُسبقاً - As for the second chapter, I have explained it already.

55. Object + Verb + Subject

الشباكَ كسر الولد - The boy broke the window.

الأموالَ يحب زيد - Money, Zaid likes.

الحقَّ قال الشاهد - The truth the witness said.

56. Adjuncts + Verb + Subject

في الحديقة جلس الضيوف - In the garden, the guests sat.

فجأةً توقف القطار - Suddenly, the train stopped.

مساءاً سيصل الوفد - In the evening, the delegation will arrive.

بعد ساعات من إسقاط القوات البحرية الأمريكية في الخليج طائرة ركاب إيرانية ، مما أدى الى مصرع ٢٩٨ شخصاً أصدرت وزارة الخارجية الأمريكية أوامرها للسفارات والقواعد العسكرية في شتى أنحاء العالم باتخاذ إجراءات حراسة مشددة

Hours after the shooting down of an Iranian airliner by the American Navy in the Gulf which led to the death of 298 people, the American State Department issued orders to American military bases and embassies all over the world to take extra security measures.

57. Subject Complement + Subject

قليلة هي الموضوعات المرسومة - Few are the drawn topics.

مفيد جداً هذا الكتاب - Very useful is this book!

جميل هذا الجو - Beautiful is this weather!

رائع كلامك - Wonderful are your words.

1.4.1 Interrogative Nominal Structure الجُملة الإسميَّة الإستفهاميَّة

58. كم / هل / مَنْ / اين / لماذا . . . إلخ *+ Subject*

أين محطة القطار رجاءاً؟ - Where is the train station, please?

كم الوقت رجاءاً؟ - What is the time, please?

هل أنتِ مُستعدَّةٌ ؟ - Are you ready?

1.5 Complex Sentence Structure تركيب الجُملة المُعقَّدة

Complex sentences are traditionally those involving subordination (embedding) as in the following patterns:

59. Verb + Subject + أنَّ *+ Subject-First Sentence*

In this structure, the main clause starts with verbs like (قال - said; ذكر - mentioned, stated; صرَّح - announced; أكَّد - stressed; أوضح - explained), the subordinate clause is introduced by the particle (إنَّ/أنَّ), and the nominal subject must appear before the verb. This structure is prototypical of news reports, as in:

وأوضحت الوكالة أنَّ الطائرة غادرت المطار في تمام الساعة العاشرة صباحاً - The agency explained that the airplane left the airport at 10am exactly.

وأضافت الوكالة أنَّ قوات الإنقاذ إنتشلت مائة جثة من ضحايا الطائرة - The agency added that the rescue services picked up 100 of the airplane victims' bodies.

يعلم سالم أنَّ الوضع سيتحسن - Salim knows that the situation will improve.

نعرف أنَّ الطلاب يدرسون بجد - We know that students are working hard.

ذكرت الصحف أنَّ رئيس الوزراء سيحضر اجتماع القمة - The press said that the Prime Minister would attend the summit.

60. Verb + Subject + أنَّ *+ Subject + Subject Complement*

أخبرني سالم بأن الأمر بسيط - Salim told me that the matter is simple.

يعرف الجميع بأن التعاون مهم - Everyone knows that cooperation is essential.

61. Verb + Subject + أنْ *+ Verb-First Sentence*

إقترح المدير أنْ يبدأ المؤتمر عصراً - The manager suggested that the conference should start in the afternoon.

قرَّرت إيمان أنْ تدعو جميع صديقاتها الى حفلة زواجها - Eman decided to invite all her friends to her wedding party.

يأمل الجميع أنْ تسود العدالة - Everyone hopes that justice prevails.

أخشى أنْ يتأخر الوفد - I am worried that the delegation may arrive late.

يخاف زيد أنْ يذكر القصة الحقيقية - Zaid is scared to tell the true story.

أودُّ أنْ أدعوكم جميعاً - I want to invite all of you.

Subordinating particles, such as (عندما - when, قبل - before, etc.), introduce clauses which are part of a complex structure. The subordinate clause itself is not necessarily a complex structure (unless it has further clauses embedded in it). So:

[أخبرني بشيءٍ] [He told me something.] is a simple sentence.

[[أخبرني [بأنه سيستقيل]] [He told me [that he would resign]] is a complex sentence.

[[[أخبرني [بأنه سيستقيل [عندما ينهي عقده]]] [He told me [that he would resign [when his contract finished]]] is a complex sentence with a complex clause inside it.

The subordinating particles which introduce clauses that are part of a complex structure are like:

عندما – *when*

رجاءاً أخبر هدى عندما تراها مساء اليوم - Please tell Huda when you see her tonight.

يتعرقل السير عندما تسقط الثلوج - The traffic gets chaotic when snow falls.

قبل – *before*

سأذهب إلى المصرف قبل أنْ أحضر الإجتماع - I shall go to the bank before I attend the meeting.

كلَّمني الوزير قبل أن يغادر الوفد - The minister talked to me before the delegation left.

بعد أن – *after*

سأذهب إلى سوق السمك بعد أنْ أسحب مبلغا من المال - I shall go to the fish market after I cash some money.

سأخبركم بعد أنْ أصل - I will inform you after I arrive.

لأنَّ - *because*

نامت هدى مبكرا لأنها تشعر بالتعب - Huda slept early because she felt tired.

رغم أنَّ / على الرغم من أنَّ / مع أنَّ - *although*

صام حسان رمضان على الرغم من أنه مريض - Hassan fasted during Ramadan although he was ill.

حكمت المحكمة بالسجن على سالم رغم أنه بريء - The court sentenced Salim to jail although he was innocent.

لكي / لأن / حتى / لـ - *in order to;* لكي لا / لئلا - *in order not to*

جاء مروان لكي يعتذر من زميله - Marwan came to apologize to his colleague.

ذهبت لتتصل بالشرطة - She went out to contact the police.

خرج علي مبكرا لكي لا يفوته القطار – Ali left early so that he would not miss the train.
خرجت مبكراً لئلا يفوتني القطار - I left early so that I would not miss the train.
كأنّ - *as though*
تحدث الإمام كأنه يريد أن يبكي - The imam spoke as though he was going to cry.
سلم عزيز على ليلى كأنه يعرفها - Aziz greeted Layla as though he knew her.

The verbs (بدأ / أخذ / جاء) can also produce complex structures in Arabic, as in:

جاء الطفل يبكي إلى أمه - The child came to his mum crying.
بدأ سالم يقص لنا حكاية طريفة - Salim started telling us a nice tale.
بدأ الإقتصاد يتحسن - The economy began to improve.

Conditional structures are also another form of complex structures. These are introduced by (إنْ / إذا / مَنْ / لو / حيثما / أينما / كلما / متى ما) which mean (if), as in:

إنْ تدرسوا تنجحوا - If you study, you will pass.
إذا تحسن الإقتصاد يفرح الشعب - If the economy improves, people will be happy.
مَنْ يكذب لا يتوفق في حياته - Whoever lies will not succeed in his life.
لو إجتهدت لنجحت - Had you worked hard, you would have succeeded.
حيثما يذهب عصام تذهب زوجته معه - Wherever Isam goes, his wife goes with him.
أينما نذهب نشاهد نفس المأساة - Wherever we go, we see the same tragedy.
كُلما أنصحه لا يصغي لي - Whenever I advise him, he does not listen to me.
متى ما تتكلم سعاد يقاطعها الآخرون - Whenever Suad speaks the others interrupt her.

Relative pronouns such as (الذي / التي / الذين) also introduce complex structures in Arabic. A relative pronoun introduces clause modifying a noun, as in:
إعتقلت الشرطة الرجل الذي سرق سيارتي - The police arrested the man who stole my car.

1.6 Parenthetical Structure الجُملة الإعتراضيّة

A phrase, as an extra explanation, can be inserted within the main structure. In basic transitive/intransitive sentence structures as well as in derived structures, this phrase can be added after a subject, a direct object or an indirect object. This extra phrase can also be added after subject in equative structures, as in:

ولا يريد أحد – رغم وجوده وسط الكوبري – أن يلقي عليه نظرة .

Nobody wanted - although he was standing in the middle of the bridge - to look at him.

كان الفريق المصري – الذي دخل البطولة وهو المرشح للفوز بها – الوحيد الذي فاز بمبارياته الثلاث في الدور الأول بالبطولة .

The Egyptian team - which entered the championship and which was the candidate for winning it - was the only team which won all its first matches in the first leg of the championship.

وصل زيد – الطالب الجديد – الى الحفلة مبكراً - Zaid, the new student, arrived early to the party.

زيد – الطالب الجديد – وصل الى الحفلة مبكراً - Zaid, the new student, arrived early to the party.

رأيت زيداً – الطالب الجديد – مع زوجته - I saw Zaid, the new student, with his wife.

أعطت هدى الكتاب – الذي اشترته الإسبوع الماضي – الى خالد - Huda gave the book, which she bought last week, to Khalid.

أعطت هدى خالد – الطالب الجديد – كتابها - Huda gave Khalid, the new student, her book.

زيد – الطالب الجديد – مدرس متقاعد - Zaid, the new student, is a retired teacher.

Practical Exercises

تطبيقات

1. Provide basic sentence structures using the verbs (إستدرج ، صرَّح ، أصدر ، خطب ، أخَّر، إستجوب ، مزح ، حزن ، قَلَقَ ، إبتسم).

2. Change the basic sentence structures you have made above into derived structures.

3. Put either the basic or the derived sentence structures you have made above into both the negative and the imperative.

4. Use the verbs (طرد ، إستثمر ، سافر ، أصدر ، صدَّر) in sentences with (لكي لا / لئلا).

5. Use the verbs (سمع ، وصل ، نام) in sentences with (إلاَّ) or (ماعدا).

6. Use the verbs (كلَّم ، سرع ، صافح ، نافس ، إعتذر ، سبح) in imperative and negative imperative patterns.

7. Use the verbs (أسَّس ، حرق ، كسر ، ناقش ، إنتخب) in the passive and then in periphrastic passive structures.

8. Use the verbs (تأخر ، نجح ، أكل ، إعترف ، إستشار) in complex structures with (بعد أنْ ، لانَّ ، رغم أنَّ ، حتى ، كأنَّ ، قبل أنْ).

9. Use the verbs (نصح ، نجح ، إعترف) in complex structures with relative pronouns which introduce clauses modifying nouns.

10. Use the adjectives (عليم ، كبير ، قليل ، سهل ، حريص ، مطَّاط ، مفيد ، ليِّن) in comparative structures.

11. Use the verbs (إنكمش ، نفع) in comparative structures.

12. Use the following expressions in comparative patterns and use them in sentences:

أقوى ، أجمل ، أضخم ، أسهل ، أحلى

13. Provide the comparative form for the following words: كبُر ، عَلِم ، قلَّ

14. Provide the comparative form with nominalization for the following words and use them in effective Arabic: إنكمش ، تمطَّى ، تساهل ، علم ، حرص

15. Use the extraposing device (أما . . . فـ) with the verbs (أجَّل ، بقى ، جدَّد ، إستقبل ، إشترى) to provide derived sentences (see structure 54).

16. Underline the basic and derived sentences in the following text:

إتهم العراق مجدداً السفارة البولندية في بغداد التي تدير شعبة رعاية المصالح الأمريكية في العراق بإدخال مواد وأجهزة فنية ممنوعة من بينها أجهزة تعمل

بالأشعة تحت الحمراء .

وكانت حكومة وارسو قد اتهمت السلطات العراقية من قبل بفتح حقيبة دبلوماسية لسفارتها في بغداد وهو مانفاه رئيس دائرة المراسم في الخارجية العراقية .

وقد استدعت وزارة الخارجية العراقية السفير البولندي وسلمته مذكرة احتجاج رسمية شديدة اللهجة بسبب قيام السفارة بادخال الأجهزة ، واتهمت الوزارة بولندا بالقيام بتصرفات منافية لروح ونص اتفاقية فيينا لعام ١٩٦١ .

وأكد بيان الوزارة العراقية ان السفارة البولندية أدخلت في الثاني من شهر نوفمبر الماضي مجموعة من الأجهزة دون الحصول على الموافقات المحددة من الجانب العراقي ، وان السفارة قد قامت مجددا في نهاية شهر فبراير الماضي بجلب ١٤ صندوقا تحوي أجهزة فنية دون الحصول على موافقات إدخالها ، وأشار الى أن السلطات العراقية في مُجمَّع القادسية الحدودي على الحدود مع الأردن ، قد وضعت يديها في الإسبوع الماضي على أجهزة فنية عبارة عن منظومة إنذار مبكر الكترونية وأجهزة للتحكم عن بعد تعمل بالأشعة تحت الحمراء إضافة الى منظومة إتصالات هاتفية محظورة تضر بأنظمة الاتصالات المستخدمة في جميع أنحاء العراق .

ولم يذكر البيان العراقي إن كانت الإجهزة قد وردت لصالح السفارة البولندية أم الى شعبة رعاية المصالح الأمريكية في بغداد . وفي وارسو قالت وكالة رويتر للأنباء ان بولندا اتهمت العراق بانتهاك اتفاقية جنيف .

من جهة أخرى بدأت وزارة الصحة العراقية في العمل بموجب البطاقة الدوائية الجديدة للعائلات لمواجهة النقص الحاد في الأدوية . وقد أعلن المسؤلون بالوزارة أن العمل بالبطاقة الجديدة قد بدأ تنفيذه في الأول من مارس الجاري . وكانت الحكومة العراقية قد حولت أكثر المستشفيات في البلاد الى العمل بالتمويل الذاتي .

(الأهرام : ١٣ مارس ٢٠٠٠ ص ٥)

Chapter Two
Description of Lexis
وصفُ المُفردات

2.1 Classification of Vocabulary تصنيفُ المُفردات

There are two distinct classes of words:

(1) Closed Class of Words (الفئة المُغلقة للكلمات): The closed set of words are morphemes which represent the minimal unit of grammatical function and which do not have any referential meaning; i.e., they do not refer to an object or to an abstract concept. Therefore, this set of morphemes performs a grammatical function but to which we cannot add any prefixes or suffixes, and of which we cannot derive any other forms. Examples of this set are:

(i) the definite article (الـ), as in الكتاب - the book.
(ii) prepositions (حروف الجر), such as (في ، على ، من ، إلى ، نحو ، تحت ، . . .).
(iii) the plural morpheme (علامة الجمع) added to a noun or an adjective, such as:
- the dual morphemes (ـان) and (ـين) suffixed to the noun or the adjective, as in كتابان - two books, كتابين - two books, and مفيدان - useful, which are the dual of كتاب - book, and مفيد - useful.
- the broken plural morpheme which is realised by an internal vocalic change and which varies from one noun to another, as in أنهر or أنهار - rivers, كُتُب - books, أولاد - boys, سيوف - swords, رجال - men, أشهُر - months, علوم - sciences, etc., which are the plurals of (نهر ، كتاب ، ولد ، سيف ، رجل ، شهر ، علم) respectively.
- the sound masculine plural morphemes (ـون) and (ـين) suffixed to the noun or adjective, as in معلمون - teachers, and معلمين - teachers, which are the plurals of (معلم). Similarly, in adjectives we find مشهورون / مشهورين - famous.
- the sound feminine plural morphemes (ـات) suffixed to the noun or adjective, as in مدرسات - female teachers, إجتماعات - meetings, جميلات - beautiful, which are the plurals of (مدرسة ، إجتماع ، جميلة).
- zero plural morpheme which is found in words which represent either a group such as حـمَـام - pigeons, or which represent a quantity as in تمْر - dates, which are the plurals of (حمامة ، تمرة).
(iv) pronouns which include:
- free pronouns like انا - I, انتِ - you (fs), انتَ - you (ms), انتم - you (mpl), انتُنَّ

- you (fpl), نحنُ - we, etc.

- bound pronouns which are either suffixed or prefixed to a verb like the (أ) in أكتُبُ - I write, the (نـ) in نكتُبُ - We write, the (تـ) in تكتُبُ - She writes, the (ـوا) as in كتبوا - They (m) wrote, كتبن - They (f) wrote, etc.

- demonstrative pronouns like هذا - this (ms), هذه - this (fs), ذلك - that (ms), تلك - that (fs), هؤلاء - these, etc.

(v) conjunctions such as فـ ، ثُمَّ ، و - and/and then.

(vi) the two sets of إنَّ/أنَّ and كانَ.

(vii) zero tense morpheme which means that the past or present tense is not indicated by a given morpheme, as in ذَهَبَ - He went, نَجحَت - She succeeded.

(2) Open Class of Words (الفئة المفتوحة للكلمات): The open set of words is represented by lexical items which have a referential meaning and can be increased through suffixes or prefixes. This class of words includes:

- verbs such as درّس - to teach, نام - to sleep
- nouns such as كلمة - word, بنات - girls
- adjectives such as رؤوف - merciful, طويل - long
- adverbs such as بهدوء - quietly, باختصار - briefly

All types of text involve both the closed and the open class of words (see Chapter Four Text Types in Arabic). From a stylistic point of view, however, we need to focus on the open set of words. This is because they have a lexical meaning, i.e., refer to concrete objects like شجرة - tree, and عالِم - scientist, denote actions such as سَبَح - to swim, and refer to abstract notions such as سَعادة - happiness, and جمال - beauty.

2.2 Semantic Fields الحُقولُ الدلاليَّة / شبكة دلالات الألفاظ

This semantic mapping is a network of sense relations that hold between a group of words whose key concept (the nodal item) is in the middle, as in (سفارة - embassy), (حكومة - government), (مستشفى - hospital) and (رتبة عسكرية - military rank) See next two pages:

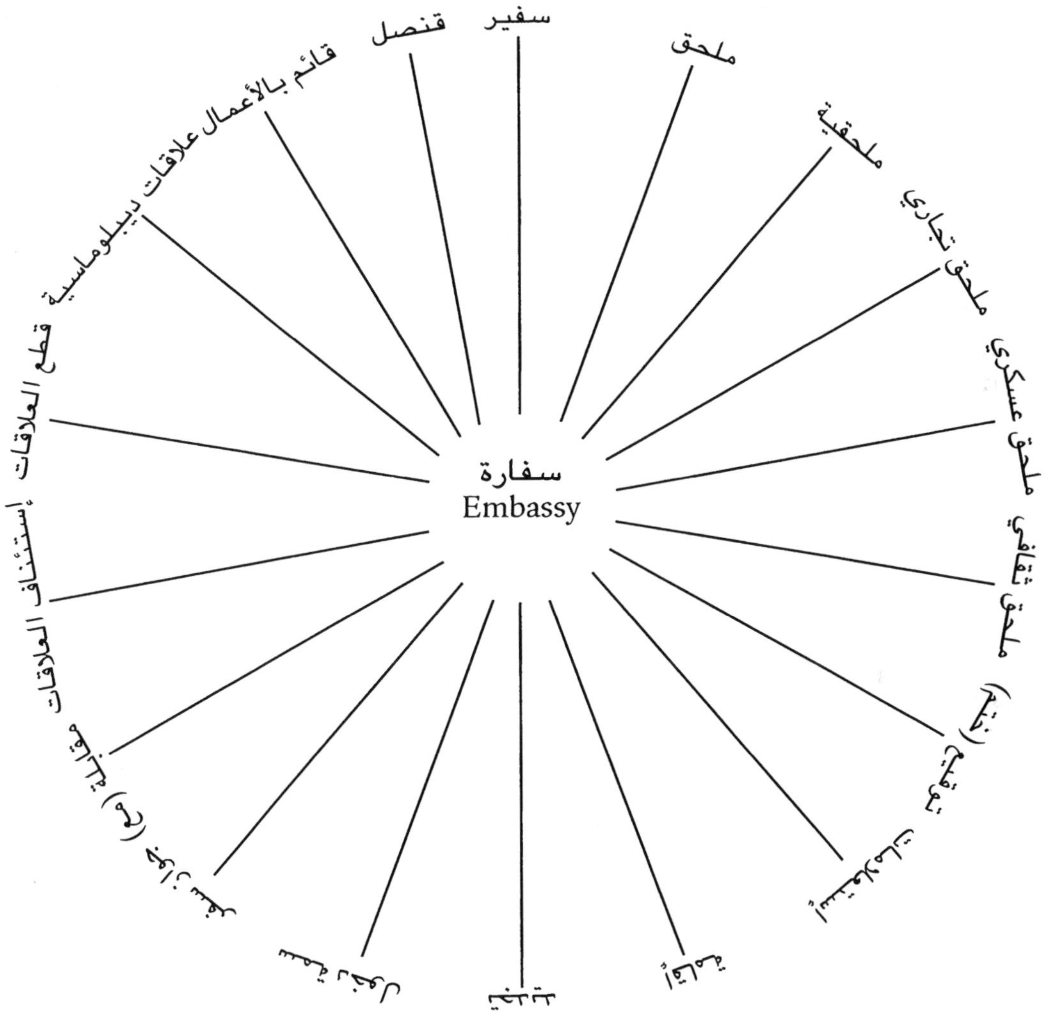
سفارة
Embassy
سفير
قنصل
قائم بالأعمال
علاقات دبلوماسية
قطع العلاقات
إستئناف العلاقات
ملحق
ملحقية
ملحق تجاري
ملحق عسكري
ملحق ثقافي

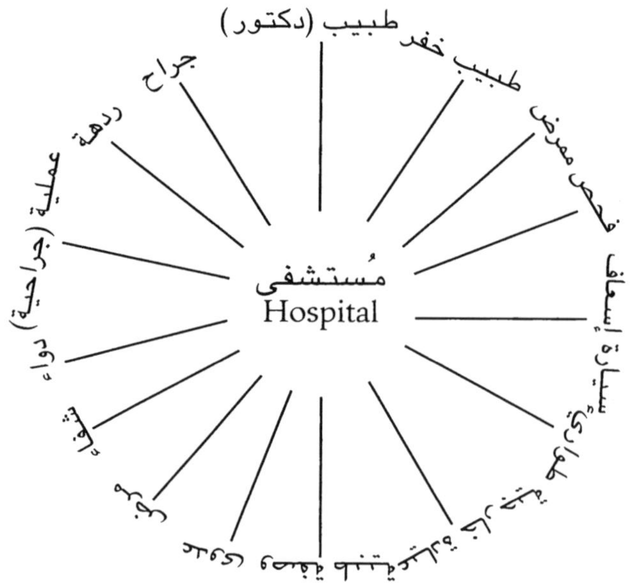

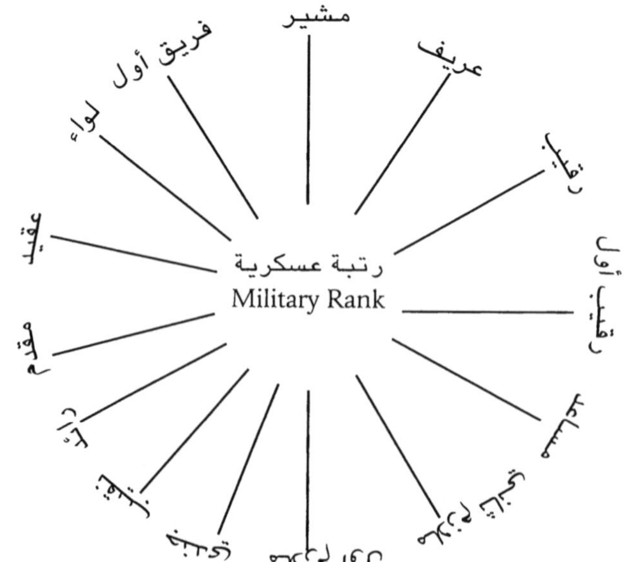

2.3 Collocation المُصاحبة اللَّفظيَّة

Words are collocationally restricted. They occur and co-exist only in conjunction with their mates in a special linguistic environment. Each individual word has its own collocative meaning. Certain verbs collocate only with certain nouns; similarly, certain adjectives collocate with certain nouns.

Verbs
(عوى - to howl) collocates with (كلب - dog) or (ذئب - wolf).
(نبح - to bark) collocates with (كلب - dog).
(دَرَّس - to teach) collocates with (أستاذ / مُعلِّم) or (أستاذة / مُعَلِّمة - teacher).

Adjectives
(فَتَّاك - lethal, fatal) collocates with (سلاح - weapon) or (مرض - disease).
(مُثَقَّف / مُثقَّفة - educated) collocates with nouns like (رجل / إمرأة - man/woman, أُمة / شعب - people/nation, إنسان / إنسانة / شخص – person).
(جائر - unjust) collocates with (قرار - decision, resolution).
(ظالم - unjust) and (مظلوم - oppressed) collocate with (شخص - a person, حاكم - a ruler, شعب - people).
(جميلة - beautiful) collocates with (إمرأة / فتاة - lady/girl).
(وسيم - handsome) collocates with (رجل / ولد - gentleman, boy)

2.4 Collocational Clashes تضارُب المُصاحبة اللَّفظيَّة

Some collocations are language-specific. Therefore, lexical collocational errors take place between speakers of different languages when they put words together in the wrong context. While in English the noun (envy) collocates with the adjective (green), in Arabic, the same noun (envy - حقد) collocates with a different adjective (أسود - black) to get (حقد أسود - 'black' jealousy) as in (وجوه مليئة بالحقد الأسود - faces 'green with envy.') Moreover, the lexical item (حقد) denotes a negative entailment in Arabic but in English it may denote a neutral entailment, as in (I really envy you. I wish I had an expensive car like yours.) (see 2.16). Another example of a perfectly acceptable collocation in English but unacceptable in Arabic is the word (heavy). This word collocates in English with: 1. rain, 2. losses, casualties, 3. fighting, 4. shelling, 5. artillery, 6. fire, 7. bombardment, 8. blow, 9. weight, 10. meal, 11. sea, 12. sleep, 13. heart, 14. industry, 15. smoker, 16. eyes, 17. traffic. In Arabic, however, the word (heavy) collocates in this English group with (artillery) to get (مدفعية ثَقيلة), (weight) to get (وزن ثقيل), (meal) to get (وجبة ثقيلة/دسمة), and (industry) to get (صناعة ثقيلة).

Consider the translations of the English collocations above into Arabic:
1. أمطار غزيرة, 2. خسائر جسيمة/فادحة, 3. قتال عنيف/ضار, 4. قصُف مكثف,

5. وزن ثقيل ,9. ضربة قاضية ,8. قصُف مكثف ,7. نيران مكثفة ,6. مدفعية ثقيلة ,
10. صناعة ثقيلة ,14. قلب كئيب ,13. نوم عميق ,12. بحر هائج ,11. وجبة ثقيلة ,
15. مرور مزدحم/إزدحام ,17. عيون نعسانة ,16. مدخن مفرط

Similarly, speakers of different languages make grammatical lexical errors. In Arabic, nouns like (معلومات ، مساعدات ، نصائح ، ضغوط ، طائرات حربية ، مياه ، سَمَك/أسماك) can collocate in the plural with other words but in English they only appear in the singular, as in:

معلومات عامة - general information
مساعدات مالية - financial aid
نصائح طبية - medical advice
ضغوط إقتصادية - economic pressure
طائرات حربية - aircraft
مياه معدنية - mineral water
سمك/أسماك - fish

While in Arabic the same adjective such as (إقتصادي ، تأريخي) collocates with different words in different contexts, in English context plays a major role in the selection of a lexical item for a specific meaning:

مؤتمر إقتصادي - economic conference
السفر بالحافلة أرخص من القطار - Travelling by coach is more economical than by train.
أماكن تأريخية - historical places
زيارة تأريخية - historic visit

Emotive words and expressions like (إستشهد - to die a martyr) and (إنتقل إلى رحمة الله - to pass away) can only collocate with emotive words like (البطل - the hero, الشجاع - the brave man) but not with other nouns like (اللص - the thief, الجبان - the coward); the expression (إنتقل إلى رحمة الله), however, can also collocate with non-emotive nouns like (والدي - my father, مديرة المدرسة - the headmistress).

The collocation of certain words overlaps sometimes, such as the word (فاسد) which can collocate with a number of lexical items like:

نظام فاسد - corrupt regime
أخلاق فاسدة - very bad manners
كلام فاسد - idle talk
عقيدة فاسدة - false faith
لحم / حليب /بيض فاسد - rotten, bad meat/milk/eggs

2.5 Collocational Range مدى المُصاحبة اللّفظيّة

Words habitually co-occur with other words to form a number of phrases or idioms. The key word is called nodal item, the words that co-occur with it are called collocates, and the rainbow of collocates for a nodal item is

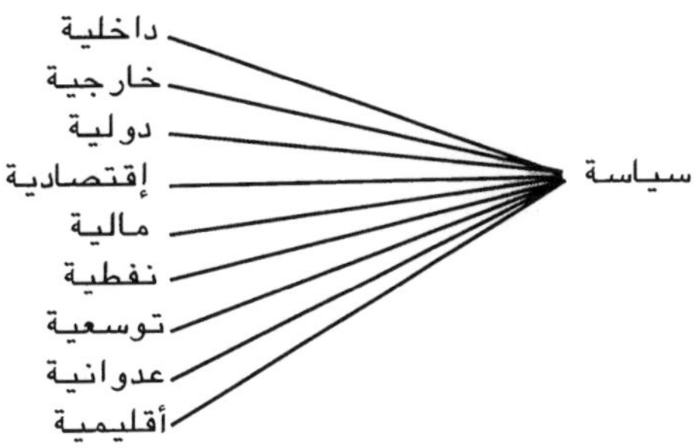

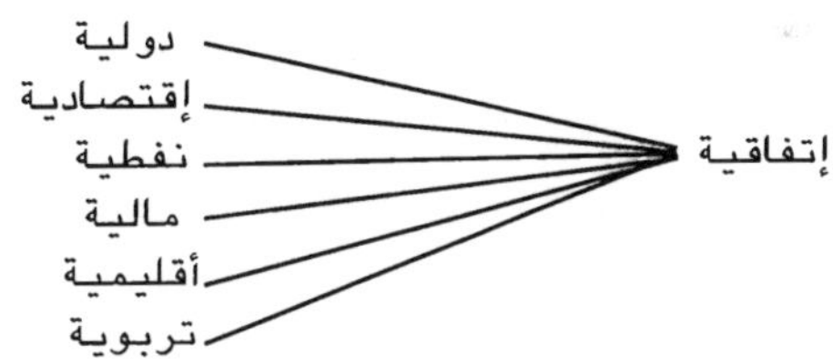

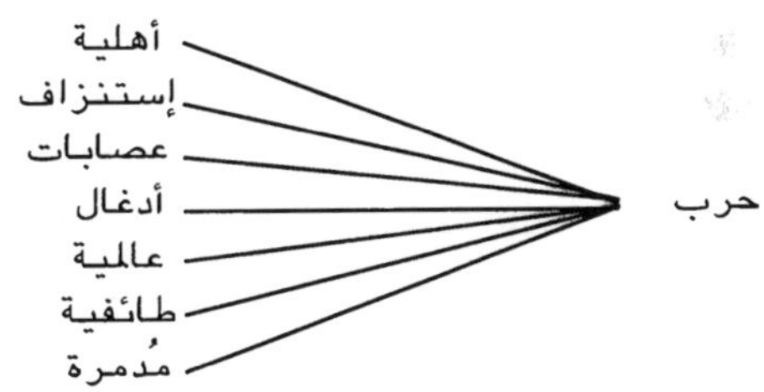

called collocational range, as in (سياسة - policy), (إتفاقية - agreement) and (حرب - war). These are nodal items whose collocational ranges, i.e., their collocates, involve a number of collocates:

As we can see, the collocational ranges of some nodal items overlap. For instance, certain collocates have co-occurred with the two different nodal items (سياسة) and (إتفاقية). These collocates are ، نفطية ، إقتصادية ، دولية)

(سياسة، مالية، إقليمية، تربوية). Therefore, the collocational range of (سياسة) overlaps with that of (إتفاقية) but the collocational range of (حرب) does not overlap with any of them.

2.6 Collocational Restrictions قُيود المُصاحبة اللّفظيّة

Words within a phrase or a clause can be described as mates. Collocational (selectional) restrictions are to do with collocational features which indicate the prohibition on permitted combinations of words in certain linguistic structures. The conditions relating to where a given word can co-occur are violated at times by language users. Collocational restrictions are broken when words are employed figuratively. However, the violation of collocational restrictions can produce unacceptable sentences although they are grammatical (see 2.7 Collocation and Grammar). Understanding the componential semantic features of a given lexical item is vital if we do not want to violate the collocational restrictions of a specific word. The verb (ضَحكَ - to laugh) has the componential features [+ Human, + Animate] which require special nouns with these features like (مريم - Mariam, المعلم - the teacher) so that they can co-occur with the verb ضحك without violating the collocational restrictions. However, when another noun with different semantic features [_ Human, _ Animate] like (الحجر - stones) or (الكلب - the dog) occurs with the same verb, the result is a figurative use of language, as in (ضحك الحجر - The stones laughed).

The collocational restrictions of verbs like (بكى - to weep, إبتسم - to smile) impose restrictions on permitted combinations with certain nouns which enjoy the componential features [+ Human, + Animate, +_ Adult] like الطفل - the child, المسافر - the passenger). However, verbs like (تخرج - to graduate, تزوج - to get married) require nouns with the semantic features [+ Human, + Animate, + Adult] like (الطالب - the student). On the other hand, verbs like (عوى - to howl) require nouns with the collocational semantic features [+ Animate, _ Human, + Canine] while verbs like (صهل - to neigh) require nouns with the collocational semantic features [+ Animate, + Equine, _ Human]. On the other hand, the verb (مات - to die) requires only [+ _ Human, + _ Adult, + Animate] nouns.

Adjectives like (مُخلص - faithful) require a noun with the collocational features [+ _ Human, + Animate, + _ Adult, + _ Male] like (رَجُل - man, إمرأة - woman, بنت - girl, ولد - boy, كلب - dog).

2.7 Collocation and Grammar المُصاحبة اللَّفظيَّة والنحو

Stylistically, the study of collocation and grammar are closely related. We have learned in Chapter One the possible structures that we may encounter in Arabic. In section 2.6 (Collocational Restrictions), we have learned that certain verbs or adjectives can only permit specific nouns (cf. 2.19 Colligation). However, language users, at times, do tend to break the collocational restrictions rule and produce grammatical but stylistically unacceptable sentences.

In this section, we need to investigate the restrictions imposed by Arabic on the co-occurrence of words within a given sentence in order to produce stylistically and grammatically acceptable structures. It is important to learn that certain verbs do not permit the occurrence of certain nouns. While, for instance, verbs like (أكل - to eat, مضغ - to chew, إشترى - to buy) permit in the same sentence nouns like (خبز - bread, لحم - meat, رز - rice, تفاحة - apple) as objects, other verbs like (شرب - to drink, تنفس/إستنشق - to breath, كسر - to break, كسَّر - to break into pieces) do not permit the same nouns above. However, the verbs (قطع - to cut, قطَّع - to break into pieces) collocate only with two of the set of nouns above (لحم ، تفاحة). Also, none of the verbs mentioned so far are compatible with abstract nouns like (سعادة - happiness, فرح - joy, معرفة - knowledge, إيمان - faith, دمار - destruction, بناء - construction).

Stylistically, we also need to be aware of the grammatical fact that the seventh form (إنفعل) of the Arabic verb system is a reflexive (intransitive) verb which does not require an object in the sentence. Verbs of this form are like (إنشقّ - to open up, إنكسر - to be broken, إندحر/إنهزم - to be defeated, إنْسَحَبَ - to withdraw, إنقطع - to break, cut off, إنغلق - to close, إنخدع - to be deceived, إنزعج - to be annoyed, إنطلق - to set off, إنطفأ - to be extinguished, إنقضى - to elapse) which can only take subject nouns like (أرض - earth, شباك - window, عدو/جيش - enemy/army, عدو/جيش - enemy/army, حبل/خط - rope/line, باب - door, فتاة - girl, صديقي - my friend, ولد - boy, ضوء/شمعة - light/candle, وقت - time) respectively.

To produce stylistically acceptable sentences, certain Arabic verbs especially in reported speech require the particle (أنّ - that) accompanied by other elements (أنّ - that + pronoun, or أنّ + noun + pronoun) such as (ذكر - to mention/say, قال - to say, أكد - to stress/confirm, صرح - to state/announce) (cf. 2.19 Colligation):

واكد الوزير أنّه سيحضر إجتماع وزراء الخارجية العرب - The minister confirmed that he would attend the meeting of Arab foreign ministers.

صرحت وزارة الخارجية المصرية أنّها ستسحب سفيرها لدى لندن - The Egyptian foreign ministry announced that it would withdraw its ambassador in London.

ذكر متحدث رسمي عراقي أنّ بلاده ستقطع تمثيلها الدبلوماسي مع بريطابيا - An Iraqi official spokesman said that Iraq would sever its diplomatic representation with Britain.

Note that stylistically acceptable Arabic sentences require anaphoric reference rather than cataphoric reference. Anaphoric reference occurs when a noun is first mentioned followed by its pronoun, as in sentence (a). Cataphoric reference, however, takes place when a pronoun occurs first followed by its noun, as in sentence (b). Stylistically, Arabic requires (favours) sentences like (a):

(a) وأكد الرئيس الجزائري في خطابه يوم أمس على الإنتخابات الحرة - The Algerian president stressed in his speech yesterday the free elections.
rather than sentence (b):
(b) وفي خطابه يوم أمس أكد الرئيس الجزائري على الإنتخابات الحرة – In his speech yesterday, the Algerian president stressed the free elections.

because in sentence (a) we have anaphoric reference in (خطابه - his speech) where the anaphora (ـه - his) comes after and refers to (الرئيس الجزائري - the Algerian president).

Certain verbs and idiomatic expressions require the occurrence of nominalization. The verb (رفض - denied, refused), for instance, takes nominalization after its subject:

رفض وزير الخارجية الصيني التعليق على تقارير من الولايات المتحدة ... – The Chinese foreign minister refused to comment on reports from the United States ...

The idiomatic expression (لم يستبعد إمكانية - he did not rule out the possibility), for instance, co-occurs with nominalization which comes after the idiom. However, the subject should occur after the verb (يستبعد), as in:

لم يستبعد وزير الداخلية الجزائري إمكانية اتخاذ قرار بحل الجبهة الاسلامية للانقاذ – The Algerian interior minister did not rule out the possibility of dissolving the Islamic Salvation Front.

The nominalization words are (التعليق) and (اتخاذ).

Expressions like (من المتوقع أنْ - it is expected; من الصعب أنْ - it is difficult to; من المرجح أنْ - it is likely that; من المفـروض أنْ - it is supposed that; من المحتمل أنْ - it is probable that) are followed by a verb-first sentence, as in:

مِن المتوقع أنْ يصل الرئيس السوري اليوم - It is expected that the Syrian president arrives today.

2.8 Word Set مجموعة كلمات

Any set of words which are associated with each other and have a semantic relation to each other has a cohesive effect and is used for textual purposes as in (سبورة - board, معلِّم - teacher, إمتحان - exam, مكتبة - library), (صحن - plate, سكينة - knife, مطبخ - kitchen, طباخ - cooker), and (شارع - road, سيارة - car , حافلة - coach/bus, رصيف - pavement, أضوية مرور - traffic lights, مكان عبور / معبر - crossing zone) where each lexical item has a semantic relation to the rest of the set, on the one hand, and also produces lexical cohesion (see 3.3.5.1 Collocation).

2.9 General Nouns أسماء عامّة

Arabic general nouns can be classified into concrete/abstract, human/non-human, and animate/inanimate nouns which can be used in any type of text to create lexical cohesion. The types of general noun which we encounter in Arabic are:

(a) concrete human nouns: أسماء بشريّة ملموسة

رجل ، زوج ، مرأة / إمرأة ، زوجة ، ولد ، بنت ، فتى ، فتاة ، صبي ، صبية ، شخص ، إنسان ، إنسانة ، المرء ، ناس ، شعب ، قوم ، أمة ، أقلية ، مخلوق ، مخلوقة ، عائلة ، أُسرة ، العرب ، المسلمون ، النصارى / المسيحيون ، اليهود

whose plural forms are:

رِجال ، نِساء ، أولاد ، بنات ، فتيان ، صبيان ، أشْخاص ، شعوب ، أقوام ، أُمم ، أقليات ، مَخلوقات ، عوائل ، أُسر

(b) abstract human nouns: أسماء بشريّة مُجرّدة

إنسانية ، بشرية ، الخلق ، إسلام ، مسيحية / نصرانية ، يهودية ، دين / ديانة ، حضارة ، عادات ، تقاليد ، زواج ، طلاق ، زفاف ، صداقة ، محبة ، مودة ، عداء ، بغضاء

Examples:

أعرف ياسين معرفة شخصية فهو رجل كريم وإنسان عبقري – I know Yasin personally. He is a generous man and a genius human being.

نعم ولكن كريمة هي زوجة وأم وموطنة بريطانية والمعروف عنها أنها إنسانة خلوقة وإمرأة مُسالمة – Yes, but Karima is a wife, a mother, and a British citizen and she is well-known for being a polite human being and a peace-loving lady.

بريطانيا بلد متعدد الحضارات فيها أديان مختلفة مثل الإسلام والمسحية واليهودية وأقليات مختلفة مثل العرب والآسيويين وغيرهم – Britain is a multi-cultural country in which there are different religions such as Islam, Christianity and Judaism, as well as different minorities such as Arabs, Asians and others.

Notice:

ياسين → رجل → إنسان

كريمة → زوجة → أم → مواطنة → إنسانة → إمرأة

بريطانيا → بلد → حضارات → أديان → إسلام/مسيحية/يهودية

أقليات → عرب → آسيويين

These words form a word set since each one has a semantic relation to the rest of the set in each sentence; similarly, each word has a cohesive function in their respective sentences (see 3.3.5.1 Collocation).

(c) concrete animate non-human nouns: أسماء غير بشريَّة حيَّة ملموسة
دودة - worm, حشرة - insect, سمك - fish, حيوان - animal, مخلوق - creature
whose plural forms are: ديدان ، حشرات ، أسماك ، حيوانات ، مخلوقات

Examples:

القطة حيوان أليف – The cat is a domesticated animal.

تعيش الأسماك في الماء ولكن قسم من هذه المخلوقات يعيش في قاع المحيط – Fish live in water but some of these creatures live in the ocean bed.

Notice:

قطة → حيوان

أسماك → مخلوقات

Similarly, there is a semantic interrelation between these words which appear in the same sentence. For this reason, these words contribute to the cohesion of the sentence.

(d) concrete inanimate non-human nouns: أسماء غير بشريَّة غير حيَّة ملموسة

مادة - substance, شيء - thing
whose plural forms are:
أشياء ، مواد

Examples:

أريد أن أشتري هذه التُحفيات - I want to buy these souvenirs
إتركها ، هذه أشياء تافهة - Leave them. These are silly things.

لا تلمس هذه القناني - Do not touch these bottles.
لماذا ؟ - Why?
لأنّ فيها مواد سامة - Because there are poisonous substances in them.

(e) abstract inanimate nouns: أسماء غير حيّة مُجرّدة
علاقة ، خُلُق ، سعادة
The plural forms of (علاقة - relation) and (خُلُق - manners) are (علاقات) and (أخلاق) respectively. There is no plural form for سعادة - happiness.

Examples:
علاقات دبلوماسية - diplomatic relations
علاقة غرامية - love relationship
علاقة مودة بين الطُّلاب - friendly relations among students
سميرة عندها أخلاق عالية - Samira has very good manners.

(f) abstract inanimate fact nouns: أسماء حقيقة غير حيّة مُجرّدة
مسألة ، قضية ، فكرة ، حقيقة ، مشكلة ، أمر ، شيء ، طبيعة / عادة
whose plural forms are:
مسائل ، قضايا ، أفكار ، حقائق ، مشاكل ، أُمور ، طباع / عادات

Examples:
زرت كردستان مؤخرا كصحفي ورأيت الفقر بعيني وأدركت بأن المسألة الكردية قضية إنسانية فهذه حقيقة ثابتة وشيء لاينكر

I visited Kurdistan recently and saw in my eyes the poverty and realized that the Kurdish issue is a human cause. This is a well-established truth and something we cannot deny.

واشتد بي الجوع وأخذت أفتش عن مكان ما وانتهى بي المطاف في مطعم قرب محطة القطار . وأخذت مكاني في الزاوية . وبعد قليل جلبت نظري شابة تطعم كلبها مما تأكل وتمسده تارة وتقبله تارة أخرى . وعزمت الخروج لكني خجلت وفكرت مع نفسي وقلت "لا ألومها . هذه طباعهم"

I was extremely hungry and started looking for any place for food. I ended up in a restaurant near the train station. I sat in a corner and after a while my attention was attracted by a young lady feeding her dog from what she was having, stroking it at one time and kissing it at another. I decided to leave but I felt embarrassed. I thought to myself and said: "I should not blame her. It is their custom".

Notice:
شيء → حقيقة → قضية → مسألة → كردستان
(تطعم كلبها مما تأكل وتمسده تارة وتقبله تارة أُخرى) → طِباع

These words also have a semantic relation to each other. The word (طباع)

refers semantically to the whole sentence (تطعم كلبها مما تأكل وتمسده تارة وتقبله تارة أخرى) (see point (iii) of 3.3.1.1 Endophoric Reference).

(g) abstract inanimate place nouns: أسماء مكان غير حيَّة مُجرَّدة
منطقة ، حي ، مكان ، مدينة
Plural forms are:
مناطق ، أحياء ، أماكن ، مدن

Examples:
A: هل سكنت في ليدز مسبقاً ؟ – Have you ever lived in Leeds?
B: لم أسمع بهذه المدينة من قبل ولكن أظن أنها مكان جميل – I've never heard of this city before but I am sure it is a nice place.

يشتهر الشرق الأوسط بالنفط ولهذا فهو منطقة حيوية – The Middle East is well-known for oil and therefore it is a strategic region.
زرنا هولت بارك وهوحي من أحياء مدينة ليدز – We visited Holt Park which is one of the areas of Leeds city.

Notice:
مكان → مدينة → ليدز
منطقة → الشرق الأوسط
أحياء → حي → هولت بارك

(h) abstract inanimate time nouns: أسماء زمان غير حيَّة مُجرَّدة
حياة ، فترة ، زمان / زمن ، وقت ، مرحلة
Plural forms are:
فترات ، أزمنة ، أوقات ، مراحل

Examples:
وقد أنهيت تعليمي الجامعي في باريس وكانت حياة شاقة ومرحلة حاسمة في شبابي
– I finished my university education in Paris. It was a very hard life and a crucial stage in my youth.

Notice:
مرحلة → حياة → تعليمي الجامعي

(i) abstract inanimate action nouns: أسماء عمل غير حيَّة مُجرَّدة
تحرك ، خطوة ، مبادرة ، رحلة ، تجربة
Plural forms are:
تحركات ، خطوات ، مبادرات ، رحلات ، تجارب

Examples:
سيتم القيام بسفرات ترفيهية خلال العطلة الصيفية والتي تعتبر مبادرة طيبة من أولياء الأمور

There will be recreational trips during the summer holidays which are considered as a good initiative by parents.

وقد قضينا إسبوعاً كاملاً في بيت بارد بلا تدفأة ولا طعام كاف . وإن كانت هذه تجربة قاسية لنا جميعاً إلاَّ أنها كانت فعلاً رحلة تحمُّل رائعة

We spent a whole week in a cold house without heating and without enough food. Although this was a harsh experience for all of us, it was in fact a wonderful endurance trip.

وقد بدأت الإدارة الأمريكية بإرسال قواتها العسكرية إلى المنطقة بينما وصفت بعض الإذاعات العربية هذه المبادرة الأمريكية بأنها تحرك مشبوه

The American administration started sending its military forces to the region while some Arab radio stations described this American initiative as a suspicious move.

Notice:

سفرات ترفيهية → مبادرة

إسبوعاً كاملاً . . . كاف → تجربة → رحلة

إرسال قواتها العسكرية → مبادرة → سياسة

(j) abstract inanimate mental nouns: أسماء عقليَّة غير حيَّة مُجرَّدة

فكرة ، منهج ، خطة ، سياسة ، خيال

Plural forms are:

أفكار ، مناهج ، خُطط ، سياسات

Examples:

أريد أن أواصل دراستي ، فما هو رأيك ؟ – I want to continue my study. What do you think?

أعتقد أنها فكرة طيبة – I believe it is a good idea.

قام حزب العمال بزيادة الضرائب ولكن البعض يرى ذلك سياسة خاطئة – The Labour party increased taxes but some people see that as a wrong policy.

Notice:

أواصل دراستي → فكرة

سياسة → زيادة الضرائب

2.10 Idioms إصطلاحات

Idioms are fixed collocations of a special kind and have a meaning as a whole. These are idiomatic expressions with a fixed order that remains unchanged. Most idioms involve the conjunction (و) while others do not, as in:

Group A المجموعة أ

السماوات والأرض – heaven and earth
ليلاً ونهاراً - day and night
أبيض وأسود - black and white
سيداتي سادتي - ladies and gentleman
جنة ونار - heaven and hell
الحق والباطل - truth and falsehood
صغاراً وكباراً - young and old
الموت والحياة - life and death
أكل وشرب - food and drink
المذنب والبريء - the innocent and the guilty
حار وبارد - hot and cold
الصادرات والواردات - exports and imports
الذهب والفضة - gold and silver
مِراراً وتِكراراً - over and over again

Group B المجموعة ب

خيانة الوعود - breach of promise
ألدول النامية - developing countries
نشرة الأخبار - the news
زير نساء - womanizer
مسألة حساسة - sensitive issue
الأمن القومي - national security
فراغ سياسي - political vacuum
بيان رسمي - official statement
الخيانة العظمى - high treason
أولياء الأمور - parents
نشرة الأحوال الجوية - weather forecast
مشعل الحرية - torch of liberty
مسألة فيها نظر - a matter that needs to be considered
وحدة الأراضي - territorial integrity
السيادة الوطنية - sovereignty
فساد سياسي - political corruption
تمثيل دبلوماسي - diplomatic representation
قطع العلاقات الدبلوماسية - severing of diplomatic relations
إستئناف العلاقات الدبلوماسية - resumption of diplomatic relations
إستئناف المباحثات/المُحادثات - resumption of negotiations/talks
حالة طواريء - state of emergency
الحزب الحاكم - ruling party
قرار تأريخي - historical decision/resolution
مغامرة سياسية - political adventure
خسائر فادحة / جسيمة - heavy losses
هجرة العقول - brain drain
إجتماع طارىء - emergency meeting
نمو إقتصادي - economic growth
منع التجول - curfew
حجة دامغة - a strong argument
قرار حاسم - decisive decision
نظام دكتاتوري - dictatorial regime
إنتصار ساحق/باهر - sweeping victory
محو الأمية - eradication of illiteracy
ظروف طارئة - emergency circumstances
تخريب إقتصادي - economic sabotage

حرب تحرير - war of liberation
حرب أدغال - jungle warfare
هجوم مفاجيء - surprise attack
حقل ألغام - minefield
منطقة عازلة - buffer zone
دليل قاطع - hard evidence
حرب عصابات - guerrilla warfare
حرب إستنزاف - war of attrition
هجوم إحباطي - pre-emptive attack
منطقة منزوعة السلاح - de-militarized zone
الحرس الوطني - national guard
تحرك مشبوه - suspicious move

Group C المجموعة ج
إنتقل إلى رحمة الله / إنتقل إلى جوار ربه / إنتقل إلى الرفيق الأعلى - to pass away
على آخر رمق - at the point of death
سَدْ رمق العيش - to keep oneself barely alive
شرب سُمّاً ناقعاً - He has had a very bitter experience
تجرّع السُّمَّ الزُعافَ - He has accepted the bitter fact

It is interesting to note that Arabic does not have phrasal verbs like English as a type of idioms like (give in) meaning (yield – إسْتَسْلَمَ).

2.11 Courtesy Expressions عبارات الإحترام

Courtesy expressions are context-sensitive where each expression has its own particular usage in terms of addressee, time and formality. These include:

السلامُ عليكم - hello (as a greeting)
وعليكم السلام / وعليكم السلام ورحمة الله وبركاته - hello (as a response to a greeting)
مع السلامة/في أمان الله - good bye
صباح الخير - good morning
مساء الخير - good evening
مرحباً - welcome (when receiving someone), or hello (when greeting someone)
أهلا ومرحبا بكم - you are welcome
أهلا وسهلا - welcome
مع السلامة / في أمان الله / نستودعكم الله - bye-bye / see you
شكراً - thank you
من فضلك - please
رجاءاً - please
رحلة سعيدة - Have a nice journey
عيد مبارك - Have a happy Eid
كل عام وأنتَ (وأنتِ) بخير / كل عام وأنتم بخير - Have a happy Eid
أسعد الله أيامكم - may God grant you happy days
عيد ميلاد سعيد - happy birthday
مبروك / ألف مبروك - congratulations
تصبح على خير - good night

2.12 Proverbial Expressions الأمثال

These are concise sayings which reflect the popular wisdom of Arabic culture, such as:

يد الله مع الجماعة - Many hands make light work.
الأقربون أولى بالمعروف - Charity begins at home.
من جدَّ وجد - No pain no gain.
لا يُلدغ المؤمن من جحر مرتين - A fox is not taken twice in the same snare.
للهرة تسع أرواح - A cat has nine lives.
الحليم تكفيه الإشارة - A wise man only needs a hint.
يوم لنا ويوم علينا - Every dog has his day.
كما تزرع تحصد - As you sow, so will you reap.
الجار قبل الدار - Ask about your neighbour before you buy the house.
الصبر مفتاح الفرج - Patience is the key to a happy ending.
التأريخ يعيد نفسه - History repeats itself.
الإتحاد قوة - Union is power.
العلم قوة - Knowledge is power.
الحب أعمى - Love is blind.
البُعد يُنسي - Out of sight, out of mind.
أعمال لا أقوال - Deeds, not words.
عصفور في اليد خير من عشرة على الشجرة - A bird in the hand is worth two in the bush.
إذا كان الكلام من فضَّة فالسكوت من ذهب - Speech is silver, but silence is gold.
ما كل بيضاء شحمة ولا كل سوداء فحمة - All is not gold that glitters.
إنكَ لا تُسمع الصُمَّ الدعاء - You are flogging a dead horse.
السلامة خير من الندامة - It is better to be safe than sorry.
في التأني السلامة وفي العجلة الندامة - More haste, less speed.
العجلة من الشيطان - More haste, less speed.
الولد سرّ أبيه - Like father, like son.
الفقر ليس عيباً - Poverty is no vice.
لا تؤجل عمل اليوم الى غد - Do not put off till tomorrow what can be done today.
أضرب مادام الحديد حامياً - Strike while the iron is hot.
للجدران آذان - Walls have ears.
عذره أسوأ من فعله - His excuse is worse than his deed.
الصديق عند الضيق - A friend in need is a friend indeed.
الطيور على أشكالها تقع - Birds of a feather flock together.
الأمور بخواتمها - All is well that ends well.
الفضولية تفتك بصاحبها - Curiosity killed the cat.
كما تدينُ تُدان - Do as you would be done by.

الحاجة أُم الإختراع - Necessity is the mother of invention.
الوقاية خير من العلاج - Prevention is better than cure.

2.13 Modes of Address صيَغُ الخطاب

Modes of address constitute a key factor in the success or failure of any interaction. Each mode of address represents a politeness formula specific for a particular person in the social, religious, or political hierarchy. Arabic is rich in honorary titles as modes of address due to the diverse social, political and religious titles in different Arab countries. These are used in both spoken and written Arabic. These include the phrases and titles of address used for a president, a king, a sultan, royal family members, ministers, ambassadors, attaches, religious and legal figures, family members, friends, and the general public:

The President - رئيس الجمهورية
_____ سيادة الرئيس _____ – Your Excellency President _____

The King - الملك
_____ صاحب الجلالة الملك – Your Majesty _____
_____ سيدي / مولاي صاحب الجلالة الملك

The Sultan - السلطان
_____ صاحب الجلالة السلطان – Your Majesty _____

Members of the Royal Family – (أفراد العائلة المالكة) الأمراء
_____ صاحب السموِ الملكي الأمير – Your Royal Highness _____
_____ سمو الأمير

Minister - الوزير
_____ صاحب المعالي – Your Excellency _____
_____ معالي الوزير
_____ الأستاذ وزير

Ambassador - السفير
_____ سعادة السفير – Mr Ambassador _____
_____ الأستاذ السفير

Attache - المُلحق
_____ سيادة المُلحق - Your Excellency the (Cultural) Attache _____

Legal and Religious Figures - رجال الدين والقضاء
_____ فضيلة / سماحة الشيخ – Your Eminence _____
_____ فضيلة / سماحة الحاكم / القاضي

Family Members - أفراد العائلة

والدي العـزيـز - Dear Father; والدتـي الـعـزيـزة / الحنـونـة / الـغـالـيــة - Dear Mother; عمـي / خـالـي العزيز - Dear Uncle; عمتـي / خـالتـي العزيـزة - Dear Aunt; جدي العزيز - Dear Grandfather; جدتـي العزيـزة - Dear Grandmother. The other adjectives used with mother (الحنـونـة - loving) and (الغاليـة - most precious) can also be used with other female members of the family, i.e., uncle and aunt. أخي العزيز - Dear Brother; أُختـي العزيزة / الحنونـة - Dear Sister.

Friends - الأصدقـاء

أخي العزيز / الأخ الأستاذ ______ – Dear ______

أُختي العزيزة / الأخت الأستاذة ______

The General Public - عامة الشعب

______ السيد / السيدة – Mr / Mrs ______

______ الأستاذ / الأستاذة

______ الأخ / الأخت - Brother/Sister ______

______ الآنسة - Miss ______

After each form of address listed above, the name of the addressee is mentioned and then followed by other expressions of respect, such as:

حفظه الله / وفقه الله / المحترم - May God grant him/her success/ the most honoured.

In Libya, however, we find different modes of address. The word (الأخ - brother) is generally used for the president, minister, or ambassador, etc. The words (رئيس - president), (رئيس الوزراء - prime minister), (وزير - minister) are not used. Instead, we find the title (الأخ) before the name of the president, as in (الأخ القـذافي - President Qadhafi). The prime minister is called (أمين اللجنة الشعبية العامة - the secretary of the general people's committee). The minister of health, for instance, is called (أمين اللجنة الشعبية العامة للصحة - the secretary of the general people's committee for health). A Libyan ambassador in an Arab country is called (أمين مكتب الأُخوَّة العربي الليبي - the secretary of the Libyan Arab brotherhood office). A Libyan ambassador in a non-Arab country is called (أمين المكتب الشعبي الليبي - the secretary of the Libyan people's office).

2.14 Military Ranks الرُتب العسكريَّة

These are special expressions used in the armed forces to signify a military rank. The following military ranks include the three arms - navy, air force, and army:

Navy البحرية	Air Force الطيران	Army الجيش	الرتبة
Admiral of the Fleet	Marshal of the AF	Field Marshal	مشير
Admiral	Air Chief Marshal	General	فريق أول
Vice-Admiral	Air Marshal	Lieutenant General	فريق
Rear Admiral	Air Vice-Marshal	Major General	لواء
Commodore (1st Class)	Air Commodore	Brigadier	عميد
Commodore (2nd Class)	Group Captain	Colonel	عقيد
Captain	Wing Commander	Lieutenant Colonel	مقدم
Commander	Squadron Leader	Major	رائد
Lieutenant Commander	Flight Lieutenant	Captain	نقيب
Lieutenant	Flying Officer	Lieutenant	ملازم أول
Sub-Lieutenant	Pilot Officer	2nd Lieutenant	ملازم ثانى
Warrant Officer	Warrant Officer	Warrant Officer	مساعد
Midshipman	Flight Sergeant	Staff Sergeant	رقيب أول
Cadet	Sergeant	Sergeant	رقيب
Petty Officer	Corporal	Corporal	عريف
Leading Seaman	Aircraftman	Lance Corporal	وكيل عريف
Ordinary Seaman	Private	Private	جندى

2.15 Connotation الدلالاتُ الضمنيَّة / المعنى المُسْتَتِر

Languages interpret the physical world differently. Some words, therefore, are culture-specific. The word (بومة - owl) in Arabic has the connotation of stupidity or bad luck. In English, however, the same word has a distinct connotative meaning which signifies knowledge, wisdom; some educational institutions, like the University of Leeds and Leeds Metropolitan University use the owl in their logos. Similarly, unlike English, the word (كلب - dog) in Arabic signifies a negative connotation which is that of (نجاسة - uncleanliness). Also, the word (فلاح - farmer) has the connotation of a poor family. While the word (girlfriend) in English has the connotation of a female who loves her boyfriend and can practise sex with him, in Arabic its counterpart (عشيقة) has the connotative meaning of *love* only and does not have the same English connotation as sex is not part of the relationship due to religious reasons.

More examples:

Word	Connotation
ثور - ox, بومة - owl	very stupid
دجاجة - chicken	coward
ذئب/أسد - wolf/lion	brave, courageous
عذراء - virgin	virtue
محجبة - lady with head scarf on	virtue
فدائي - freedom fighter	bravery and self-denial

2.16 Ameliorative and Pejorative Expressions المُفردات المُحسِّنة والإزدرائيَّة

Some words have emotive overtones. Words may express positive, neutral or negative connotative entailments. Cross-cultural entailment can influence the translations into English of some of these words. In Arabic, we have different entailments (assumptions) about the semantic implication of different words which may be morphologically related. The choice of one word or the other reflects our personal, socio-political and religious beliefs. Some of these words may be used with a negative particle like (عدم / لم). Positive, neutral and negative entailment is to do with what we assume when we use one word rather than the other. As language users, this is related to our lexical preferences which are the centre of our communicative interest. The use of a word in the wrong context will seriously affect the semantic appropriateness of the sentence. Some of these words are listed on the next page:

Positive	Negative
عمَّر / تعمير	إستعمر / إستعمار
تعاون مع / تعاون مع	تواطأ /تَواطُؤ
سأل عن/ سؤال عن	إستجوب / إستجواب إستنطق / إستنطاق
إستَفاد من / إستِفادة من	إستغل / إستغلال
كافح / كفاح	قتل / قتال
تجسَّس على / تجسُّس على	جمع (معلومات) / جَمْع (معلومات)
أخبر عن / إخبار عن	تجسَّس على / تجسُّس على
إقتلع / إقتلاع	شرَّد / تشريد
نظف / تنظيف طهَّر / تطهير	أباد / إبادة
لم يعط / عدم إعطاء	حرم / حرمان
لم يعط / عدم إعطاء	أنكر / إنكار
أقر / إقرار	إعترف / إعتراف
أخذ / أخْذ	إغتصب / إغتصاب
لم يعترف بـ / عدم الإعتراف بـ	إنتهك / إنتهاك نَقَض / نَقْض
نشر / نَشْر	سرَّب / تسرُّب
إغتال / إغتيال	قتل / قَتْل
قال / قول	لفَّق / تلفيق
دخل إلى / دخول إلى	تسلَّل إلى / تسلُّل إلى إجتاح / إجتياح غزا / غزو
إنسحب من / إنسحاب من	إندحر / إندحار إنهزم / إنهزام / هزيمة
طرَد / طرْد	هجَّر / تهجير
تَرَك / تَرْك	هَجَرَ / هَجْر
ثار على / ثورة على	إنقلب على / إنقلاب على
خطط لـ / خطة	تآمَر على / تآمُر / مؤامرة

2.17 Emotiveness المُفردات العاطفيَّة

Some words denote an emotive meaning with an emotional effect on the reader/listener. This meaning, however, is culture-bound. Therefore, some of the emotive words constitute semantic voids, i.e., culture- or language-specific lexical items whose meaning cannot be rendered into a target language by a single word but only through paraphrase. These are like (تراويح - after supper long prayers during Ramadan), (عقيقة - a party in which a lamb is slaughtered and food served for relatives and friends immediately after the birth of a baby), (زفة - very noisy night wedding celebration for both the bride and the bridegroom), (شرف - nobility/honour), (عرض - sexual honour).

Other emotive words are like عذراء/باكر - virgin, وطن - homeland, حُماة الوطن - protectors of the homeland (i.e., armed forces), نسور الجو - pilots, بطل - hero, فدائي - freedom fighter, خائن - traitor, treacherous, خيانة - treachery, غدار - traitorous, الفردوس - Paradise, جهنم - Hellfire, متطرف - extremist, قلعة - palace, طائش/مغامر - thoughtless/reckless, كرامة - dignity, ضمير - conscience/innermost, أدران - filthy legacy, as in أدران الماضي - filthy legacy of the past, أدران الإستعمار - dirty legacy of colonization.

2.18 Cultural Emotive Clash تضارُب المُفردات العاطفيَّة الحضاريَّة

Some emotive words in one language may have a negative socio-political or religious connotative/expressive meaning in another language. For instance, to an Arab, words like (فدائي ، مجاهد) are emotive words pregnant with highly positive and expressive meaning equivalent to (freedom fighter with self-denial). However, the same Arabic words, when translated into English, lose their expressive value and are usually rendered as (terrorist) or sometimes transliterated as *mujahid* for the word (مجاهد). Similarly, the word (متحررة - (female) liberal) reflects a negative emotive meaning which is that of being westernized with no respect to her religious principles. In English, however, the word (liberal) enjoys a positive expressive meaning. During the Bosnian war with the Serbs in the early 1990s, an emotive word (ethnic cleansing) emerged in British and European media. This word was used as a literal translation from an emotive Serbian expression with a connotative meaning (to cleanse Bosnia from the Muslims), i.e., 'treating the Bosnian Muslims as germs'. In Arabic, however, the same expression should be rendered as (الإبادة العرقية - ethnic annihilation) with an expressive meaning of *Muslim holocaust*. Other examples are below:

Emotive Words	Emotive Meaning in Arabic	Emotive Meaning in English
أصولي	a firm believer in Islam	fundamentalist
محجبة	a virtuous lady observing Islamic law	backwardness
إستعمار	occupation by a foreign country	managing the affairs of another country for people's own sake
إقطاعي	one with self-interest who takes advantage of farmers	landlord
عقوبات إقتصادية	injustice	justice
بومة	stupidity	wisdom
جمل	patience	no expressive meaning
رمضان	worship	no expressive meaning
تراويح	worship	no expressive meaning
لواطي	vice	neutral
سحاقية	vice	neutral

2.19 Colligation المُصاحبة النحوية

We can group a number of words as a set according to their grammatical function without considering their grammatical classes or relations. Colligations are language-specific. For instance, a set of verbs like (صرَّح - to announce, ذكر - to state/mention, أكَّد - to stress, قال - to say) take the particle (أنَّ - that); therefore, they are colligates or are in colligation with (أنَّ) sentences. Similarly, the set of verbs as colligates like (إعتمد - to depend, إحتج - to protest, كذب - to lie) require the preposition (على) and are, therefore, in colligation with the preposition (على). In English, however, these verbs cannot form a set of colligates because they require different prepositions (on, against, to) respectively. (see 2.7 Collocation and Grammar).

Another set of colligates are the verbs (مشى - to walk, ذهب - to go, غادر - to leave, سافر - to travel, وصل - to arrive) which are in colligation with the preposition (الى) meaning *to* and *at* respectively. The verb set (تحارب - to fight each other, إتفق - to agree, إنسجم - to be in harmony) colligates with the preposition (مع) meaning *against*, *on*, and *with* respectively. However, the adjective set (متفائل - optimistic, متشائم - pessimistic, منزعج - annoyed, upset) is in colligation with the preposition (مِن) meaning *about, about* and *with/at/about* respectively.

2.20 Synonyms المُرادفات

Words which signify the same meanings are synonyms. Synonymy does not mean identical meaning between two words but the two words can be used in different contexts giving a similar meaning. Examples of Arabic synonyms:

إنسحب - to withdraw/to retreat = تراجع = تقَهْقَر
بنى - to build/to construct = عمَّر = شيَّد
علَّم - to teach = درَّس = فهَّم = لقَّن = غذّى بأفكار
درَس - to study/read راجع = إطّلع على = قرأ = طالَعَ
أعطى - to give = منح = أنفق = وهب
مُجْتهد - hard working = مواضب = مُلتزم = شغول = حريص
مؤدَّب - polite, respectful of others = خلوق = يحْتَرِم = مُطيع = ذو حياء
إرادة - will/determination = تصميم = عزيمة
مُضطهَد - oppressed = مظلوم

2.21 Antonyms المُفردات المُتناقضة

Words have opposite meanings to other words, such as:

مُثقَّف/مُتعلِّم - educated/learned # جاهِل/أُمِّي/غير مُتعَلِّم - uneducated/illiterate
ذكي - clever # غبي - stupid
فضيلة - virtue # رذيلة - vice
مُتزوِّج - married (m) # أعزب - single (m)
مُتزوِّجة - married (f) # عازبة - single (f)
رجل - man # إمرأة - woman
صادق - truthful # كذّاب/كاذب - liar
مدني - civil # عسكري - military
فرحان - happy # حزين - sad
فقير - poor # غني - rich
وسيم/جميل - beautiful/handsome # قبيح - ugly
مُحافظ - conservative # مُتَحَرِّر - liberal
حار - hot # بارد - cold
حق - truth # باطل - falsehood
سلام - peace # حرب - war
صديق - friend # عدو - enemy
نظام - order # فوضى - chaos

2.22 Hyponyms المُفردات ذات الترابُط الدلالي

Hyponymy is the relationship that exists between specific and general words where the meaning of the specific word is included in the meaning of the general word. In other words, words are members of a lexical class. Therefore, the specific word is referred to as a hyponym while the general word is called a superordinate. The set of words (حمل - lamb, خروف - sheep, نعجة - ewe, كبش - ram, كبش مخصي - wether) are the co-hyponyms of the superordinate term (خروف - sheep); similarly, each word of the same set is a hyponym of the same superordinate term.

The terms (كرسي - chair, كرسي بلا ظهر - stool, أريكة - sofa, سرير - sofa) are the co-hyponyms of the superordinate (أثاث - furniture).

The terms (تفاحة - apple, برتقالة - orange, ليمونة - lemon, كمثرى - pearl, خوخ - peach, أناناس - pineapple, رمان - pomegranate, عنب - grapes, موز - banana, تمر - dates, رقي - watermelon, بطيخ - melon) are the co-hyponyms of the superordinate term (فاكهة - fruit).

Also the words (شارع/طريق - street/road, زُقاق/ممشى/جادّة - alley, ممر/سبيل - pathway, طريق مسدود - cul-de-sac, شارع فرعي - lane, طريق خارجي - motor way, طريق مُعلق - flyover) are the co-hyponyms of the superordinate term (طريق - street/road).

Similarly, a set of verbs like (مشى / جرى / سار - to walk, هرول / ركض - to run, أسرع - to be quick, to hurry, ذهب / إنطلق - to go, أتى - to come, ساق - to drive) are all co-hyponyms of the superordinate verb (ذهب - to go).

2.23 Polysemes المُفردات مُتعدِّدة المعاني

A polyseme is a word which has several meanings (cf. homonyms below), as in:

سائلٌ : *1. the one who asks (a question or when in need) 2. liquid*
1. سأجيب السّائل مهما كان سؤاله - I shall answer the one who asks whatever his question is.
2. هل الزئبق سائل ؟ - Is mercury a liquid?

ظرف : *1. envelope 2. a circumstance*
1. وضعت الرسالة في الظرف - I put the letter in the envelope.
2. مررت بظروف قاهرة - I have been through very difficult circumstances.

2.24 Homonyms المُفردات المُجانسة

Homonyms are words which happen to have the same phonological form but different meanings, as in:

ساعة : *1. time 2. watch*
1. الساعة العاشرة - It is ten o'clock.
2. عندي ساعة رقمية - I have a digital watch.

ورقة : *1. a paper 2. leaf*
1. أحتاج ورقة واحدة - I need one paper.
عندي عدة أوراق نقدية - I have many bank notes.
2. تسقط الأوراق في الخريف - Leaves fall in Autumn.

دقيق : *1. accurate 2. flour*
1. عملي دقيق - My work is accurate.
2. أحتاج أن أشتري دقيق - I need to buy flour.

2.25 Acronyms المُفردات المَنْحوتة / المُفردات الأوائليَّة

An acronym is a combination of the initial letters of a number of words that can be pronounced as an independent word. It is a shortened form of a number of words which can stand on its own and be used as an independent lexical item, such as (حماس) which stands for (حركة المقاومة الإسلامية). Some foreign acronyms have also become loan words in Arabic, such as:

طائرة الأواكس - EWACS (Early Warning Aircraft System) منظومة طائرات الإنذار المبكر
صاروخ سام - SAM (surface-to-air missile) صاروخ أرض – جو
الجيا - GIA (Groupe Islamic Arme) الجيش الإسلامي للإنقاذ
اليونسكو - UNESCO (United Nations Educational, Scientific, and Cultural Organization) منظمة التربية والعلم والثقافة التابعة لهيئة الأمم المتحدة
اليونيسيف - UNICEF (United Nations Children's Fund) صندوق رعاية الطفولة التابع لهيئة الأمم المتحدة
الناتو - NATO (North Atlantic Treaty Organization) حلف شمال الأطلسي

2.26 Calques مُفردات / عبارات مُترجَمة حرفياً

These are loan translations of foreign words into Arabic. Calques are a kind of borrowing through the direct translation of foreign words into Arabic, such as:

قطار الأنفاق - underground, the tube
مصعد/سُلَّم كهربائي - lift
ناطحة سحاب - skyscraper
جيوب مقاومة - pockets of resistance
أسلحة الدمار الشامل - weapons of mass destruction

قاذفة صواريخ متعددة - multiple rocket launcher
ناقلة أشخاص مدرعة - armoured personnel carrier

فرِّق تسُد - divide and rule	مسودة قرار - draft resolution
مركبة فضاء - space craft	طائرة تجسُّس - spy plane
الطائرة الشَّبح - stealth fighter	نقَّال/جوَّال - mobile phone
قناة فضائية (الفضائيات) - satellite channel	قطَع غيار - spare parts
مكوك الفضاء - space shuttle	جولةَ مكوكية - shuttle diplomacy
عملية السلام - the peace process	فتح حساب - open an account
حصة الأسد - lion's share	مخزون ذهب - gold reserve
عُملة صعبة - hard currency	جسر معلَّق - suspension bridge
قمَّة موسعة - extended summit	إجتماع موسع - extended meeting

إلقاء الكرة في ملعب فلان - to throw the ball into X's court

قضية موضع خلاف - a controversial matter (issue)	ألغام أرضية - land mines
قضايا عالقة - pending matters	إنفجار سُكاني - population explosion
مقهى الإنترنت - internet cafe	حرب أسعار - price war
قائمة فحص - checklist	العقل المدبر - the master mind
مكافأة نقدية - cash reward	دار إستراحة - guest house
قوة تدخُّل سريعة - rapid reaction force	تُجَّار حرب - war lords
الوضع الراهن - status quo	حرب إستنزاف - war of attrition
تحكُّم عن بُعُد - remote control	عُنق الزجاجة - bottleneck
خصخصة - privatization	جمهوريات الموز - banana republics
تبييض الأموال - money laundering	قسم الأفراد / الذاتيَّة - personnel

2.27 Loan Words and Neologisms المُفردات الدخيلة والمُستعارة

Contacts with other cultures and languages have led to the borrowing of foreign words into Arabic, such as:

باص - bus	تلفون - telephone
كتلي - kettle	كراج - garage
تلفزيون / تلفاز - television	فيديو - video
راديو - radio	كليشة - cliche
بلوز - sweater	بنطلون - trousers
جينز - jeans	سوبرماركت - supermarket
رادار - radar	هلكوبتر - helicopter
ستاد - stadium	بترول - petrol
غاز - gas	واير - wire

أكسجين - oxygen
كاربون - carbon
فيروس - virus
جنرال - general
دكتور - doctor/PhD holder
باراسيتيمول - paracetamol
ستراتيجية - strategy
سايكولوجية - psychology
بسكت - biscuits
إنترنت - internet
تلغراف - telegraph
أوتوماتيكي - automatic
دراماتيكي - dramatic
ترام - tram
بار - pub
كاميرا - camera

نتروجين - nitrogen
بنسلين - penicillin
ميكروب - microbe
كابتن - captain
بروفسور - professor
شيزُفرينيا - schizophrenia
تكتيك - tactics
كيك - cake
هيتر - heater
بيجر - pager
فيتامينات - vitamins
قناة - canal
بارومتر - barometre
بوليس - police
سندويش - sandwich

A new loan word (كانتون - canton) has appeared as a headline on Monday 3 April 2000 in Al-Hayat daily and has been used in the dual case:

عبد ربه : إسرائيل تقترح لدولة فلسطين كانتونين مُحاصرَين يربط بينهما ممر
(الحياة : ص ١ الإثنين ٣ أبريل (نيسان) ٢٠٠٠)

Although some of the above foreign loan words have been replaced by modern standard Arabic neologisms, the same old forms of loan words are still used by ordinary Arab speakers and by the media. However, the rest have continued in their current use in Arabic. For instance, the loan word (بروفسور) is still used in formal/informal written and spoken modern Arabic although a neologism for it has been coined which is (أستاذ كُرسي). The foreign loan words which have been replaced by modern Arabic neologisms are like:

باص is replaced by حافلة (bus/coach)
تلفون is replaced by هاتف (telephone)
كتلي is replaced by سَخَّان (kettle)
كراج is replaced by مرأب (for both keeping or maintaining the car). It is also replaced by ورشة تصليح سيارات (for maintaining/servicing the car).
تلفزيون is replaced in Syria by الجهاز المرئي المسموع and in Libya by الإذاعة المرأية (television)
بنطلون is replaced by سروال
راديو is replaced by مذياع (radio)

هلكوبتر is replaced by طائرة عمودية / سمتية (helicopter)
ستاد is replaced by ملعب كرة القدم (stadium)
بترول is replaced by نفط (oil)
واير is replaced by سلك (wire)
جنرال is replaced by فريق أول (General)
كابتن is replaced by رئيس الفريق (captain of a football team) and by نقيب (captain in the army)
دكتور is replaced by طبيب (medical doctor)
شيزوفرينيا is replaced by إنفصام الشخصية (schizophrenia)
سايكُولوجية is replaced by نفسية (psychology)
كيك is replaced by كعكة (cake)
بيجر is replaced by جهاز إستدعاء هاتفي (pager)
تلغراف is replaced by برقية (telegraph)
أوتوماتيكي is replaced by تلقائي (automatic)
دراماتيكي is replaced by جذري (dramatic)
بارومتر is replaced by محرار (barometre)
بوليس is replaced by شرطة (police)
بار is replaced by خمّارة / حانة
كاميرا is replaced by جهاز تصوير

2.28 Grammatical Forms الأشكال النحويّة

One of the striking features of Arabic stylistics is the employment of certain words of special grammatical forms. These are the absolute object, active participle, passive participle, and parallelistic forms. The use of these grammatical forms contributes in the realization of an effective style and the elevation of impact on the reader/hearer.

- *Absolute Object forms* (المفعول المُطلق) are formed by repeating the same verb in the form of its verbal noun in order to add an extra force to the verb, as in:

فاز حزب العمال فوزاً ساحقاً في الإنتخابات العامة – The Labour Party won a landslide victory in the general elections.
وأخذ يتكلم كلاماً لا معنى فيه – And he started talking nonsense.
نجحتُ نجاحاً باهراً في الإمتحانات – I achieved excellence in my exams.
بكى بُكاء الطفل – He cried like a baby.
تمرض مرضاً لاعلاج له – He is ill with an incurable disease.
عارضْتُه معارضة شديدة – I opposed him strongly.
نمت نوماً عميقاً – I fell fast asleep.

- *Active Participle forms* (إسم الفاعل) usually have the pattern (فاعل) which signifies the doer of an action. Active participles enjoy the force and effect of a verb. However, they are considered as nouns or adjectives since they can take the plural form, as in:

هو قائد عظيم – He is a great leader.
هو لاعب محترف – He is a professional player.
العمال يساهمون مساهمة فعَّالة في النمو الإقتصادي – Workers play a significant role in economic growth.
إجتمع القادة العرب في القاهرة – The Arab leaders met in Cairo.

- *Passive Participle forms* (إسم المفعول) usually have the pattern (مفعول) which signifies the person or thing that is the direct object of an action; therefore, the passive participle is commonly used in impersonal sentences where the direct subject is not stated. The passive participles are also considered as nouns or adjectives since they can take the plural form, as in:

قال المتهم أنه بريء – The suspect said that he was innocent.
أجريتُ مقابلة مع المحكوم عليه بالإعدام – I made an interview with the one who is sentenced to death.
ما المطلوب مني ؟ – What is required of me?
كان المرحوم رجلا طيبا – The deceased was a nice man (i.e., the one, whom I wish God will send His mercy on him, was a nice man.)

- *Parallelistic Structure forms* (عبارات متوازية التركيب) are those which have the same structural rhythmical pattern employed for a stylistic effect, as in:

هم الذين نهبوا ثرواتنا وسلبوا أموالنا وأخذوا علومنا – It was they who looted our fortune, robbed our money, and took our sciences.
عندي إذن حُسن تدبير وسلامة تفكير – I have got then good management and sound reasoning.
ليس في كلامي إمتهاناً ولا إنتقاصاً لحقوق المرأة – There is nothing in my speech that degrades or belittles women's rights.

Practical Exercises
تطبيقات

1. Provide the semantic fields for (محادثات) and (دروس).
2. Provide the collocates for (إنسان) and (بلد) and then underline the items that overlap between these two words.
3. What are the collocational restrictions of (تسلّق), (بكى), (عادل), and (نبح)? Give the words that can co-occur with each word.
4. What are the nouns that usually collocate with the verbs (وقّع) and (طبخ)? Provide some sentences for each verb.
5. What are the verbs that usually collocate with the nouns (أشجار) and (جريدة)? Provide sentences for each verb.
6. What is the word set of (روضة أطفال), (حفلة), and (الأمم المتحدة)?
7. Provide the synonyms of (صعب), (يحكم), (تحدث), (أستاذ), (رؤوف), and (إقتتال).
8. Provide the antonyms of (محبة), (مغلق), (سائل), (كسول) and (حق).
9. Provide the co-hyponyms of the superordinate word (مركبة).
10. Provide the active and passive participles of the verbs (قتل), (كتب), (قرأ), (حفر), and (صاد) and use each one in a sentence.
11. Provide the absolute objects of the verbs (مسك), (حبَّ), (قال), (إندحر) and (خطب) and use them in sentences.
12. Identify the type of the general nouns in the following text:

لنتفق بداية على أن العلم لايقتصر على معرفة الفيزياء والكيمياء والطب وإنما هو المعرفة بشتى أنواعها . لذلك فإن قيمة الشعوب فيما تنتج من علوم وتنظيمات ومواد وقيم ، وهي عوامل أساسية أربعة ، وثيقة الصلة فيما بينها . كما أن فقر أي أمة من العلم هو أمر رديف وملازم لفقرها من المادة . واليوم يكاد يكون من المستحيل التعامل مع أي مجتمع معاصر بدون التوفر على زاد معرفي تتصاعد متطلباته يوما بعد يوم .

إن الرقابة التي تمارسها الدولة الاستبدادية على الانتاج الثقافي ظاهرة معروفة بما فيه الكفاية . لقد ساهمت هذه الرقابة ولاتزال في إجداب العقل العربي وتصحُّر ثقافته وانخفاض مستوى أدائه ناهيك عن بروز ظاهرة غريبة لم يعرفها الوطن العربي في أحلك فترات تأريخه . إنها الصعوبة المتزايدة لتنقل الكتب والافكار في عصر تميز بسهولة المواصلات وسرعتها . لقد أنبتت سياسة دولة الاستبداد على الفصل بين الثقافة وبين العلم . وكانت الدولة تتوهم أنها تدعم

بهذا فكرها . بهذه الحالة من الاهتراء المتسارع للقيم والقانون والعلم والعمل يدّعي البعض أننا بصدد التقدم والحال أننا ندور في حلقة مفرغة ونعمق يوماً بعد يوم تبعيتنا على المستوى الشخصي في الداخل وتبعيتنا كشعوب وأمة تجاه عالم خارجي غربي أو آسيوي جعل من الفاعلية ومن توفير شروطها همه الاول .
(منصف المرزوقي – الاستقلال الثاني : ١٩٩٦ ص ٤٤)

Chapter Three
Text Structure
هيكلُ النَّص

3.1 What is a Text? ما معنى النَّص؟

The text refers to any written or spoken passage of any length. However, it cannot be just a random collection of sentences neither can the sentences be just a random collection of lexical items. The text should be a unified whole whose units - words and sentences - are connected together in a cohesive manner through cohesive devices that make the text hang together and create its unique texture and total unity. In each text, the cohesive devices are employed as linguistic means intra-sententially (within the same sentence) and inter-sententially (between sentences) to achieve cohesion.

3.2 What is Cohesion? ما معنى التَّماسُك النَّصي؟

Cohesion refers to the cohesive devices which are regarded as major linguistic features of any text that are used to bind the units of the text together. Arabic has its own cohesive devices which are used as linguistic resources to achieve cohesion in all Arabic text types. The various types of cohesive ties in Arabic include reference, substitution, ellipsis, conjunction, and lexical cohesion. The cohesive devices of reference, substitution, ellipsis, and conjunction refer to grammatical or semantic relations, while the cohesive device of lexical cohesion refers to lexical relations. Due to the fact that Arabic and English are two incongruous languages there will be limits of translatability of the examples provided; the lexical items used for cohesion in Arabic may not be equivalent to those in the English version. The cohesive devices in Arabic are discussed below.

3.3 Types of Cohesion أنواع التَّماسُك النَّصي

3.3.1 Reference الإشارة

Reference items in Arabic are the pronouns which identify for us the person or thing spoken about. Reference is the relationship between a word and its pronoun; it, therefore, signifies a semantic relation. In Arabic, pronouns refer to persons, things, and places. Items of reference in Arabic can be classified into endophoric and exophoric.

3.3.1.1 Endophoric Reference الإشارة ضمن النَّص

Endophoric reference applies to someone/something within the text as it has been explained above where different pronouns within different texts refer to different people, things, or places. In other words, the text helps us to retrieve the information about what a specific pronoun refers to. In Arabic, the types of reference which are text-bound are:

(i) personal reference (الإشارة بالضمائر الشَّخصيَّة) which is realized by personal pronouns. Pronouns in Arabic are either detached (منفصل) such as (هو - he, هي - she, هم - they, etc.) or attached (متصل) which can either be attached to a verb like (تَ - you (2ms), ت - you (fs), ـوا - they (3mpl), (ن - they (3fpl), etc., a noun like (ـه - his), (ـهَا - her/hers), (ـهم - their/theirs (m)), etc., or a preposition like (ـه - him), (ـها - her), (ـهم - them (m)), etc.

Examples:
هو طالب - He is a student.
هي طالبة - She is a student.
هم طلاب - They are students.

بيته جديد - His house is new.
بيتها جديد - Her house is new.
بيتهم جديد - Their house is new.

أخذت منه الكتاب - I took the book from him.
أخذت منها الكتاب - I took the book from her.
أخذت منهم الكتاب - I took the book from them.

(ii) general reference (الإشارة بالكلمات العامة) which is realized by the reference items like (آخر - another one (ms), آخرون - other ones (mpl), أُخرى - another one (fs), أُخريات - other ones (fpl), الأول - the first (ms), الأولى - the first (fs), أحدهم - one of them (ms), إحداهن - one of them (fs), etc., whose reference is to a person, thing or place.

Examples:
ويُذكر أن منظمة الإغاثة الإسلامية قد أرسلت شُحنتين من الأغذية إلى ألبانيا الأولى عن طريق البر والأخرى عن طريق البحر

Human Relief Organization has sent two consignments of food to Albania, one by land and the other by sea.

ولاحظت أن الرئيس الفلسطيني أبو عمار ركز على نقطتين طوال النهار : الأولى أن المجلس الوطني الفلسطيني صوت على كنفدرالية مع الأردن ، والثانية هي أنه في كل مرة تحدث عن القرارين ٢٤٢ و٣٣٨

I noticed that the Palestinian President Abu Ammar stressed two points throughout the day: the first was that the Palestinian National Congress voted for a federal union with Jordan, and the second was that he always talked about the two resolutions 242 and 338.

وقد تجمعت أمام المبنى الأمهات مع أطفالهن وكانت إحداهن تهتف "العار لبلير"

In front of the building, mothers with their children gathered and one of them was shouting "Shame on Blair".

ولم يلق أحد اللوم على نفسه

No one put the blame on himself.

(iii) extended reference (الإشارة بالضمير المُوسَّع) is realized by reference items like (هو/ هي , هذا / هذه and ـه / ـها). The reference item (ـه / ـها) are usually suffixed to one of the particles (إنَّ / أنَّ). Extended reference items do not refer to a person, thing, or place which is already mentioned in the text; they instead refer to a portion of text which is already mentioned and which represents a fact, as in:

Example 1:

وينبغي أنْ يحتل تعاطي المخدرات خاصة بين الأشخاص دون السن القانوني أولوية بين المواضيع المدرجة في جدول أعمال مؤتمر الشرطة السنوي لأنها مشكلة القرن الحادي والعشرين .

Drug taking, especially by underage people, should be given priority among the items on the agenda of the annual police conference. It is the problem of the 21st century.

Example 2:

واعتبر دبلوماسي مصري أن نقل إجتماع وزراء الخارجية العرب إلى بيروت رمزي . انه رسالة إلى إسرائيل تؤكد أن كل العرب متضامنون مع لبنان .

An Egyptian diplomat regarded the transfer of the Arab foreign ministers' meeting to Beirut as symbolic. It was a message to Israel confirming that all the Arabs have solidarity with Lebanon.

Example 3:

واشتد بيَ الجوع وأخذت أفتش عن مكان ما وانتهى بيَ المطاف في مطعم قرب محطة القطار . وأخذت مكاني في الزاوية . وبعد قليل جلبت نظري شابة تطعم

كلبـهـا مما تـأكل وتمسـده تـارة وتـقـبـلـه تـارة أُخـرى . وعـزمـت الخـروج لكنـي خـجلت وفكرت مـع نفسـي وقلت "لا ألـومـهـا . هـذه طبـاعـهـم".

I was extremely hungry and started looking for any place for food. I ended up in a restaurant near the train station. I sat in a corner and after a while my attention was attracted by a young lady feeding her dog from what she was having, stroking it at one time and kissing it at another. I decided to leave but I felt embarrassed. I thought to myself and said: "I should not blame her. It is their custom".

In the first example, the extended reference made by (ـها - it) of (لانـهـا) refers to the portion of text (تـعـاطـي المخدرات خـاصـة بـين الأشـخـاص دون الـسن الـقـانـونـي). Also, in the second example, the extended reference made by (ـه - it) of (إنه) refers to the portion of text (إجـتـمـاع وزراء الخـارجـيـة الـعـرب الـى نـقـل بـيـروت). In the third example, the extended reference (هذه - it) refers to the portion of text (شـابـة تـطـعـم كلبـهـا مما تـأكل وتمسـده تـارة وتـقـبـلـه تـارة أُخـرى). All the portions of texts have already been mentioned in the same text and all represent facts (see point (f) abstract inanimate fact nouns of 2.9 General Nouns).

(iv) demonstrative reference (الإشــارة بـإسـم الإشــارة) which is realized by demonstrative pronouns, such as (هـذا - this (ms)), هـذه - this (fs), ذلـك - that (ms), تـلك - that (fs), هـؤلاء - these (m/f), هـنـا - here, هـنـاك - there), etc.).

Examples:

وسـار كل شـيء حـسب الخطة المرسـومـة . فـفـي الـبـدايـة يـجـتـمـع المدعـوون فـي مكان محـدد ثم يـنـطـلـقـون إلـى مـبـنـى البـلـديـة حـيث يـنـتـظـرهـم مـوظـفـو عـقـد الـقـران . وهـنـاك يـدخل الـوالـد مـتـأبـطـاً ذراع ابـنـتـه كي يـسـلـمـهـا إلـى زوجـهـا أمـام أعـين الجـمـيـع

Every thing moved according to the designed plan. In the beginning, guests meet at a designated place and then move to the municipality building where the civil servants of the marriage contracts are waiting for them. There, the father enters arm in arm with his daughter so that he hands her in to her husband.

هـذا كـتـاب نـافـع – This is a useful book.

وذهـبـنـا الى شـاطـيء الـبـحـر . هـنـا يـنـسـى الإنـسـان هـمـومـه – And we went to the beach. Here one forgets his worries.

(v) comparative reference (الإشـارة بـكـلـمـات المُقـارنـة) which is realized by reference items like (آخـر - another (ms), (آخـرون / آخـريـن - other/others (mpl)), (أُخـرى - another (fs)), and (أُخـريـات - other/others (fpl)) and by comparative words like (أكـثـر - more/most, أقل - fewer/less, أفـضـل / أحـسـن - better, أسـوء -

worse, أجمل - more/most beautiful, etc., بشكل أسوأ / أفضل / أحسن - in a bad/better way).

Examples:

ساعات ديلما . الأكثر تميزاً . صناعة سويسرة – DELMA watches. The most distinguished. Swiss made.

وأمسك بكتفيها ونظر في عينيها وهزَّها وردَّد "أنْتِ أجْملُ ما في الدُّنيا" – He held her shoulders tightly, looked into her eyes and said: "You are the most beautiful (lady) in the whole world."

وردَّت عليه بغرور قائلة : "لقد وافقت الزواج منه لأنه ثري ويملك أكثر من نصف مليون جنيه . فكم عندكَ؟" فأجابها مطأطئاً رأسه : "عندي أقل"

She replied with arrogance: "I have agreed to marry him because he is wealthy and has more than half a million pounds. How much do you have?" He replied while lowering his head: "I've got less."

Comparative reference can also be employed in Arabic for the comparison of two persons, things, or places which may be like or unlike each other. In Arabic, comparative reference can be realized by comparative words which occur either on their own, such as (مختلف / غير - different, نفس - same, متماثل / مماثل / متشابه - identical/similar) or within a prepositional phrase, such as (بشكل / بطريقة / على نحو مماثل (متماثل /متشابه) - identically, بشكل / بطريقة / على نحو مختلف - differently), as in:

فهما نظامان متماثلان من حيث السياسة الخارجية – They are identical regimes in terms of their foreign policy.

وإنْ كانا توأمين إلاَّ أنهما يتصرفان بطريقة مختلفة تماماً – Although they are twins, they behave differently.

ولكن اقتراحك هذا هو غير الذي اخبرتني به سابقاً – But your proposal now is different from the one you told me before.

هذه طريقة مختلفة – This is a different method.

Comparative reference in Arabic can also be realized by special comparative expressions which also perform a cohesive function; these are like (على حد سواء - equally, على خلاف ذلك - on the contrary, خلافاً لـ - contrary to, بخلاف - unlike/contrary to, وإلاَّ - otherwise):

وفور معرفته لوجبة الطعام التي لا يفضلها ، صرخ بوجهها ورائحة الخمر تفوح من فمه : "أُخرجي من البيت وإلاَّ طلقتُكِ !"

Immediately after realizing that the meal served was not his favourite, he shouted in her face with the smell of alcohol coming out of his mouth: "Get out of the house, otherwise I shall divorce you!"

In the above examples, we are comparing between two regimes, twins, proposals, methods, and actions.

(vi) anaphoric reference (الإشارة بالضمير اللاحق لإسمه) is realized when a noun is mentioned first then followed by its pronoun. This is the prototypical grammatical norm in Arabic, as in:

وقد مُنِعَ الصحافي جمال كامل مِنْ مزاولة مهنته – The journalist Jamal Kamil was not allowed to practise his profession.

دخلت المُدرِّسة ومعها حقيبة مليئة بالكتب – The teacher came and with her was a bag full of books.

In the above examples, the nouns (جمال كامل) and (المُدرسة) are first mentioned and then followed by their relevant anaphoric reference items (ـه - his) and (ـها - her).

(vii) cataphoric reference (الإشارة بالضمير السَّابق لإسمه) is not the stylistic norm in Arabic; it is realized when a pronoun is mentioned first before the noun it refers to, as in:

في مؤتمر صحافي إحتفالاً بفوزهم الساحق قال الإصلاحيون أن حركتهم ظاهرة محلية

In a press conference celebrating their overwhelming election victory, the Reformists said that their movement was a regional phenomenon.

ومن جانبه ، جدد رئيس الوزراء اللبناني سليم الحص أمس نفيه وجود إتصالات بين لبنان وإسرائيل

On his part, the Lebanese Prime Minister, Salim Al-Hus, reiterated his denial of any contacts between Lebanon and Israel.

أكاد لا أُصدق ذلك . لقد باع كل ما يملك لكي يشتري خبزا لأطفاله

I do not believe this. He sold all his possessions just to buy bread for his children.

In the above examples, the cataphoric reference is represented by the cataphoric pronouns (هم - their) (ـه - his), and (ذلك - this) which have appeared before their relevant nouns (الإصلاحيون - the Reformists), (رئيس الوزراء اللبناني سليم الحص - the Lebanese Prime Minister Salim Al-Hus) and (باع كل ما يملك لكي يشتري خبزا لأطفاله) .

Therefore, the use of Arabic reference items in all the above examples is text bound where the information about the identity of each pronoun or reference item is retrievable from the text itself.

However, we have fixed expressions with cataphoric reference realized by the particle (مَنْ - who) which does not refer to any preceding noun, thing, place or portion of text, such as:

مَنْ جدَّ وجد - He who works hard succeeds.
مَنْ طلب العُلى سهر الليالي - He who wants high status sleeps less.

3.3.1.2 Exophoric Reference الإشارة خارج النَّص

Exophoric reference in Arabic, however, applies to someone/something outside the text. In other words, through the context of situation, we are able to identify the person/thing and retrieve the information about what a given pronoun refers to. A song said in a birthday or Eid party gathering contains an exophoric reference:

عيدَكْ / عيدكْ مْبارَكْ ياحَبيبي عيدَكْ / عيدِكْ مْبارَكْ ، عيدَكْ / عيدِكْ مْبارَكْ يا عيني عيدَكْ / عيدِكْ مْبارَكْ

Happy birthday (or Eid) to you my darling, happy birthday (or Eid) to you my precious one.

In this example, we are not told to whom the (كَ / كِ - you (m/f)) refers. However, we can still retrieve the referential meaning and the accurate information from the context of situation where every participant in the gathering knows the identity of the person which is signalled by the pronoun (كَ / كِ - you (ms/fs)).

Other pronouns also occur in Arabic for exophoric (situational) reference within a given context of situation, as in:

Example 1

وأخذ ينظر بدهشة على التحفيات وصمت قليلاً ثم قال : كم كلَّفك هذا ؟

He started looking with astonishment at the souvenirs; he paused and then said "How much did this cost you?

Example 2

واشتد بي الجوع وأخذت أفتش عن مكان ما وانتهى بي المطاف في مطعم قرب محطة القطار . وأخذت مكاني في الزاوية . وبعد قليل جلبت نظري شابة تطعم كلبها مِمَّا تأكل وتمسده تارة وتقبله تارة أُخرى . وعزمت الخروج لكني خجلت وفكرت مع نفسي وقلت "لا ألومها . هذه طباعهم"

I was extremely hungry and started looking for any place for food. I ended up in a restaurant near the train station. I sat in a corner and after a while my attention was attracted by a young lady feeding her dog from what she was having, stroking it at one time and kissing it at another. I decided to leave but I felt embarrassed. I thought to myself and said: "I should not blame her. It is their custom".

The context of situation tells us that the demonstrative pronoun (هذا - this) refers to (التُّحفيَّات - the souvenirs) in the first example and (هذه - it) refers to (شابة تطعم كلبها مما تأكل وتمسده تارة وتقبله تارة أُخرى - a young lady feeding her dog from what she was having, stroking it at one time and kissing it at another) in the second example. Therefore, the use of these pronouns in such examples is context bound because the information about the identity of pronouns is retrievable from the context of situation.

3.3.2 Substitution الإستبدال

We can substitute lexical expressions of any size such as a word, phrase, or clause by other lexical items. The result is a different wording rather than a different meaning. Substitution, therefore, is a lexico-grammatical relation that holds between two lexical items within a text. In substitution, the substitute lexical items are used explicitly in the sentence as markers for the substituted parts. There are three types of substitution: nominal, verbal, and clausal.

3.3.2.1 Nominal Substitution إستبدال إسمي

Nominal substitution occurs when a noun phrase is replaced by another noun such as (واحد / واحدة - one; نفس (الشيء / الأمر / الشخص) - the same (thing/matter/person); غير - different one, some more; آخر / أُخرى - another, different one(s); مثل - like; ذلك ، كذلك / هكذا - like that, so; لي / ملكي - mine), as in:

Example 1:
قميصي الأبيض وسخ . أُريد أن ألبس واحداً نظيفاً – My white shirt is dirty. I want to put on a clean one.

Example 2:
وهل عنده شُقق فخمة ومُؤثَّثة في لندن ؟ – Does he have de-luxe furnished flats in London?
نعم ، عنده واحدة في هايد بارك . – Yes. He has got one in Hyde Park.

Example 3:
هل عندكَ ساعات رقميَّة ؟ – Do you have digital watches?
نعم . كم واحدة تريد ؟ – Yes. How many (ones) do you want?

Example 4:
ماذا تأمُر ياأُستاذ ؟ – What do you want to order, sir?
رُز مع فاصوليا رجاءاً – Rice with beans, please.
وأنتَ ؟ – And you?
نفس الشيء – The same.

Example 5:
وماذا كان جوابكَ ؟ – And what was your response?
إنه إدعاء كاذب – That they were simply false allegations.
وأنت ياكريمة ؟ – And what about you, Karima?
نفَس الشيء – The same.

Example 6:
تركتم الثلاجة مفتوحة ولهذا فسد الحليب واللحم . نحتاج أنْ نشتري غيرها – You left the fridge open and that was why the milk and the meat went bad. We need to buy some more.

Example 7:
ألا تريد قلمكَ ؟ – Don't you want your pencil?
لا ، عندي غيره – No, I've got another one.

Example 8:
أشتريت قبل يومين هذا القلم ولكنه مكسور فهل من الممكن أنْ أستبدله بآخر ؟ – I bought this pen two days ago but it was broken. Can I replace it with another one?

Example 9:
هناء إمرأة جادة ولهذا أصبحت محامية ناجحة ولو درستِ بجد لأصبحتِ مثلها .
– Hana is a serious woman and that is why she has become a successful lawyer. Had you studied hard, you would have become like her.

Example 10:
مؤخراً أصبحت الأُمور معقدة والحياة صعبة جداً ولكن بصراحة لم تكن هكذا من قبل
– Recently, things have become complicated and life has become very difficult but frankly it was not like that before.

Example 11:
فهي شابة متفائلة والإبتسامة مرسومة على فمها دائماً وهي مازالت هكذا طيلة بقائها معنا
- She is an optimistic young lady and the smile is always on her lips.

She has been like that throughout her stay with us.

Example 12:
هذا كتابي – This is my book.
لا . هذا لي – No. This is mine.

In examples one, two and three, the words (واحدة ، واحد) are substitutes for the noun phrases (ساعات رقمية ، شقق فخمة ومؤثثة في لندن ، قميصي الأبيض), in examples three and four, the word ((نفس (الشيء)) substitutes the noun phrases (رُز مع فاصوليا) and (إنه إدعاء كاذب), in example seven, the word (غير) substitutes the noun (قلم), in example eight, the word (آخر) substitutes the noun phrase (هذا القلم), in example nine, the word (مثل) substitutes the noun phrase (محامية ناجحة), in examples ten and eleven, the word (هكذا) substitutes the noun phrases (الأمور معقدة والحياة صعبة جدا) and (شابة متفائلة والإبتسامة مرسومة على فمها دائما) respectively, and in example twelve, the word (لي - mine) substitutes the noun phrase (كتابي - my book).

3.3.2.2 Verbal Substitution إستبدال فعلي

Verbal substitution takes place when the whole verb phrase is substituted by lexical items like (نفس ، ذلك ، كذالك ، هذا – so, this, same); these lexical items may occur in phrases like (إن صح ذلك / إن كان الأمر كذلك / إذا كان هذا صَحيحاً - if so), as in:

Example 1:
لقد ذكروا لي بأنكَ تشجع سلمى على الإستقالة وتريد الزواج منها . – I was told that you were encouraging Salma to resign and that you wanted to marry her.
صدقني هذا غير صحيح – Believe me this is not true.

Example 2:
ولهذا علينا أنْ لا نسرف وأنْ نُطَبِّق ما نقول . فما رأيكم؟ – Therefore, we should not be wasteful and should practise what we preach. What do you think?
سنفعل ذالك . – We'll do that.

Example 3:
هل ترى أنه من الضروري التطرق إلى هذا الأمر الآن ؟ – Do you think it is necessary to refer to this matter now?
لا أظن ذلك – I think so.

Example 4:
ويعتقد المحللون الغربيون أن ليبيا متورطة فعلاً بحادث إنفجار لوكوبي وإنْ صح

ذلك فإنها ستواجه عقوبات إقتصادية صارمة .
Western analysts believe that Libya is in fact involved in the Lockerbie bombing. If so, it will face severe economic sanctions.

Example 5:
أُريد شاياً مع قدح ماء رجاءاً – I want tea and a glass of water, please.
وأنا كذالك – And so do I.

Example 6:
يا سمير ، أُكتب الصفحة الأولى إلى الصفحة الخامسة وأجب على الأسئلة باختصار
– Samir, write down from page one to page five and answer the questions briefly.
وأنا ؟! – And what about me?!
وأنتَ كذالك – You, too.

Example 7:
أخبرني بأنه سيغادر إلى الإمارات الإسبوع القادم – He told me that he would go to the Emirates next week.
زوجته ذكرت لي نفس الشيء – His wife told me the same thing.

In example one, the word (هذا) substitutes the verb phrase (verbal clause) (أنك تشجع سلمى على الإستقالة وتريد الزواج منها), in examples two, three and four, the word (ذلك) substitutes the verb phrases (أن لا نسرف وأن نطبق ما نقول), (أنه من الضروري التطرق إلى هذا الأمر الآن) and (أن ليبيا متورطة فعلا بحادث إنفجار لكوبي) respectively, in examples five and six, the word (كذلك) substitutes the verb phrases (أريد شايا مع قدح ماء) and (أكتب الصفحة الأولى إلى الصفحة الخامسة وأجب على الأسئلة بأختصار) respectively, and in example seven, the word (نفس) substitutes the verb phrase (أنه سيغادر إلى الإمارات الإسبوع القادم).

3.3.3 Ellipsis الحذف

Ellipsis is a grammatical relation. It is the omission of a part of a linguistic structure. The ellipted part, however, can be recovered from the context. Ellipsis helps us to minimize redundancy and produce a succinct and stylistically more effective structure. Although ellipsis and substitution are similar, in elliptical sentences we do not find substitute words as markers like (واحد ، نفس ، غير) for the ellipted lexical items. Ellipsis, therefore, involves no substitution at all. The ellipted element reminds us of what has already been mentioned. Ellipsis, therefore, also has a cohesive impact upon the text and is of two types: nominal and verbal.

3.3.3.1 Nominal Ellipsis الحذف الإسمي

Nominal ellipsis is ellipsis within the noun phrase, as in:

وكنت آخر من دخل قاعة الإمتحان . وفور بدئي الإجابة على الأسئلة إنكسر قلمي ولم أملك غيره .

I was the last one to enter the exam hall. Once I started answering the questions, my pen broke and I did not have another one.

من هو أفضل كاتب عربي ؟ – Who is the best Arab writer?
طه حسين – Taha Hussein.

وكيف أنت الآن ؟ – And how are you now?
أفضل – Better.

أين المُحاضرة ؟ – Where is the lecture?
في القاعة ١٧ – In room 17.

هل تشرب شاي أم قهوة ؟ – Do you want tea or coffee?
أُفضل شاي ، رجاءاً – I prefer tea, please.

هل من المُمكن أن أستعير قلمكَ ؟ – Is it possible to borrow your pencil?
أيهما تريد الأحمر أم الأسود ؟ – Which one do you want, the red or the black?
أُريد الأسود ، رجاءاً – I want the black, please.

وستكون المباراة القادمة مساء يوم الجمعة بين فريق الشباب والجزيرة وكلاهما مرشحان لبطولة آسيا .

The next match will be on Friday night between al-Shabab and al-Jazeera teams and both of them are candidates for Asia championship.

هل وصل الطلاب ؟ – Have the students arrived?
لم يصل أحد منهم . كلهم غابوا – None of them has arrived.

سأعود إلى مكتبي بعد العاشرة بعد ذلك سألتقي بنجم وخالد . – I'll come back to my office at 10 and after that I'll meet Najim and Khalid.
ولكن كلاهما بانتظارك منذ الساعة التاسعة والنصف . – But they have been waiting for you since 9.30.

وقد وصلت إلى بغداد شاحنتان من الأدوية الأولى من دولة الإمارات والثانية من عُمان . – Two trucks of medicine have arrived Baghdad, the first from the United Arab Emirates and the second from Oman.
والتقى الرئيس الفلسطيني ياسر عرفات بالوفدين كل على حدة . – The Palestinian President, Yasir Arafat, received the two delegations each separately.
من الأفضل أن تزرع الأشجار الخمسة في الحديقة الأمامية . – It is better to plant the five trees in the front garden.
ولكن سأزرع الأخرى أيضاً . – But I'll plant the others, as well.

عندي أربعة إخوة أحدهما قُتِلَ في حرب الخليج . – I have four brothers. One of them was killed in the Gulf war.

كان عندها أحلى المجوهرات لكن كلها سُرقت . – She used to have the most beautiful jewelry but all of it was stolen.

هذا الكتاب هو الأسهل والأفضل . – This book is the easiest and the best.

أكملنا الفصول الأولى التي كانت سهلة وسأشرح الصعبة في الفصل الدراسي القادم .
– We have finished the first chapters which were easy. I shall explain the difficult ones in the next semester.

3.3.3.2 Verbal Ellipsis الحذف الفعلي

Verbal ellipsis is ellipsis within the verb phrase, as in:

Example 1:
هل تحتاج أي خدمة ؟ – Do you need any service?
لا شكراً – No, thanks.

Example 2:
أيهما تفضل ؟ – Which one do you prefer?
كلاهما – Both.

Example 3:
هل أعددت الطعام ؟ – Have you prepared the meal?
نعم – Yes.

Example 4:
هل كنتَ نائم ؟
– Have you been asleep?
لا ، جالس – No, awake.

Example 5:
متى سيكون الإمتحان ؟ – When is the exam going to be?
الخميس – Thursday.

Example 6:
من قال لكَ هذا ؟ – Who told you that?
عثمان – Uthman.

Example 7:
ومن سيخبر والديه بذلك ؟ – And who is going to tell his parents?
أنا – I will.

Example 8:
هذه هي شروطي فهل توافقين ؟ – These are my conditions. Do you agree?

ربما– Maybe.

Example 9:

أظن أنه من الممكن أن نتصل بها أولاً ونأخذ رأيها فما هو رأيكَ ؟ – I think we can contact her first and take her opinion. What do you think?

نعمْ مُمكن – Yes, we can.

Example 10:

وكيف قضيت حياتكَ إذاً ؟ – And how did you spend your life, then?

مشرداً – Homeless.

Example 11:

أي حزب ستنتخب ، العمال أم المحافظين ؟ – Which party are you going to elect, Labour or the Conservatives?

لا هذا ولا ذاك – Neither of them.

Example 12:

ومتى ستباشر في عملك الجديد ؟ – And when will you start your new job?

قريباً – Soon.

Example 13:

هل أنهيت مقالتك ؟ – Have you finished your essay?

تقريَباً – Almost.

Example 14:

لقد أخبرته بكل التفاصيل ولم يعر أي اهتمام ؟ – I have told him of all the details but he did not care.

صحيح ؟ – True?

Example 15:

وأين تدرس ؟ – And where do you study?

في جامعة ليدز – In the University of Leeds.

Example 16:

هل نجح زياد وحارث ؟ – Have Ziyad and Harith passed?

نعم ، كلاهما – Yes, both of them.

Example 17:

هل وصل منير وفارس ؟ – Have Munir and Faris arrived?

لا ، لا منير ولا فارس – No, neither of them.

Example 18:

ستحضر هدى حفلة التخرج – Huda will attend the graduation party.

أكيد ؟ – Really?

Example 19:
إتركني لحالي رجاءاً – Please, leave me alone.
طيب ! – Fine!

Example 20:
هل أخبرتني بهذا مسبقاً ؟ – Have you told me about this already?
طبعاً – Of course.

Example 21:
متى ستذهب ؟ – When will you go?
في العاشرة والنصف ؟ – At half past ten.

Example 22:
من كسر الشباك ؟ – Who broke the window?
لا أدري – I do not know.

Example 23:
قررت أن أسكن في هذه الشقة . – I have decided to live in this flat.
لماذا ؟ – Why?

Example 24:
أحرجتني بهذا السؤال . – You have embarrassed me with this question.
آسِف – Sorry.

Example 25:
من الذي نشر كتابه في باريس ؟ – Who published his book in Paris?
الدكتور يوسف إبراهيم – Dr Yusuf Ibrahim.

Example 26:
ماالذي تريده مني ؟ – What do you want from me?
التحدث إليك – To talk to you.

Example 27:
ألا تجلس معنا ؟ – Won't you sit down with us?
صدقني مشغول جداً – Believe me I am very busy.

Example 28:
هل حضرت الإجتماع ؟ – Did you attend the meeting?
لا – No.

Example 29:
وكيف تشعر الآن ؟ – And how do you feel now?
أفضل – Better.

Example 30:
. أريد أن أتوقف عند هذه النقطة – I want to stop at this point.
ونحن كذلك – So do we.

Example 31:
وهل ضحكت عندما سمعت القصة ؟ – And did you laugh when you heard the story?
على العكس . بكيت – On the contrary, I cried.

Indirect responses also involve ellipsis, as in:

Example 32:
وهل تود الذهاب معهم ومخالطتهم ثانية ؟ – And do you wish to go out and mix with them again?
. إلاّ إذا سمحت لي بذلك – Only if you allow me to do so.

Example 33:
هل بإمكانك إنقاذي من هذه المشكلة ؟ – Can you get me out of this problem?
إن كنت مستعدة – If you are willing.

Analysis of the above examples:

The ellipted verbal clauses in the above examples are: in example 1 (أحتاج أي خدمة), in 2 (أُفضل), in 3 (أعددت الطعام), in 4 (كنت جالس), in 5 (سيكون أن الإمتحان), in 6 (قال لي هذا), in 7 (سأخبر والديه بذلك), in 8 (أوافق), in 9 (نتصل بها أولا ونأخذ رأيها), in 10 (قضيت حياتي), in 11 (سأنتخب), in 12 (أنك أخبرته بكل), in 13 (أنهيت مقالتي), in 14 (سأباشر في عملي الجديد), in 15 (أدرس), in 16 (نجحا), in 17 (وصلا), in 18 (التفاصيل ولم يعر أي إهتمام), in 19 (أتركك لحالك), in 20 (أخبرتك بهذا مسبقا), (ستحضر هدى حفلة التخرج), in 21 (سأذهب), in 22 (من كسر الشباك), in 23 (قررت أن تسكن في هذه الشقة), in 24 (أحرجتك بهذا السؤال), in 25 (نشر كتابه في باريس), in 26 (أريد), in 27 (نريد), in 28 (لا أجلس معكم), in 29 (لم أحضر الإجتماع), in 30 (أشعر الآن أفضل), in 31 (أن نتوقف عند هذه النقطة), in 32 (عندما سمعت القصة), (سأذهب معهم وأخالطهم ثانية), and in 33 (بأمكاني إنقاذك من هذه المشكلة).

3.3.4 Conjunction الربط / الوصل

Conjunction is a semantic relation which refers to the process in which words or sentences are systematically connected. Stylistically, Arabic is a polysyndetic language. Conjunctive elements between words or sentences are cohesive devices which are used to maintain the logical relationships among various events or situations. There are four types of conjunction; these are additive, adversative, causal, and temporal.

3.3.4.1 Additive Conjunction الربط الإضافي

Additive conjunction refers to the addition relationship between what has been said and what is to come. The typical Arabic additive conjunctive element is (و - and). Additive conjunctive elements can be employed for a rainbow of reasons: The additive conjunctive element (أو - or) is used when we speak of alternative things. The additive conjunctive elements like (إضافة إلى ذلك / علاوة على ذلك - besides, moreover, من جانبه / من جهته - on his part, جدير بالذكر - it is worth mentioning, وبطبيعة الحال - actually, naturally) are used for emphatic effect when talking about the same situation or event. The additive conjunctive elements (من ناحية ثانية ، من جهة أخرى ، على صعيد آخر - on the other hand) are used for emphatic effect when talking about a different situation or event which is related to the first one and which adds more information about it. The use of these elements adds more information about the same event or situation but from a different perspective. The additive conjunctive elements (أيضا ، كذلك ، كما أنّ - also, للسبب نفسه - by the same token) can be used for simple additive conjunction. Arabic additive conjunctive elements which can be used in a negative relationship are (أما . . . أو - either . . . or, لا . . . ولا - neither . . . nor). Additive conjunctive elements like (بالمناسبة ، على فكرة - by the way) are used to establish an afterthought relationship between sentences. When we provide examples to explain things, we can use additive conjunctive elements like (مثلا ، على سبيل المثال - for example). When we explain things, we use additive conjunctive elements like (وبتعبير آخر ، بعبارة أخرى - in other words).

Example 1:

وأضاف المتحدث قائلا أن المحادثات كانت مثمرة فعلاً . – And the spokesman added that the talks were indeed fruitful.

It should be noted that we encounter in Arabic saturated use of the cohesive conjunctive element (و - and) between two or more words or phrases, inter-sententially, intra-sententially, and between paragraphs, as in:

Example 2:

دافع الرئيس السوداني عمر الشريف بشدة يوم أمس عن قراره فرض حالة

الطواريء وحل البرلمان وتشكيل حكومة جديدة وقال أنه كان ضرورياً لتوحيد القيادة وإعادة الإنضباط في البلاد وأكّد أنه تلقى دعماً من ضباط في الجيش والشرطة وأنهم باركوا القرارات ووصفوها بأنها جاءت متأخرة .
وأوضح البشير في مؤتمر صحافي أمس أنه . . .
واستهل الرئيس السوداني في اللقاء مع الصحافيين بشرح الظروف . . .
وأجاب البشير على سؤال من الأهرام . . .
ونفى حدوث إعتقالات . . . وأكد إلتزام الأجهزة الأمنية والعسكرية بالتوجيهات . . . ونفى ما تردد من إشاعات أن . . . وأعلن أن الحزب الحاكم "بحاجة إلى كثير من الإصلاح في نظامه السياسي . . "
(الحياة : ص٥ الثلاثاء ١٤ كانون الأول (ديسمبر) ١٩٩٩)

The conjunctive (و) is used intra-sententially between phrases:
(إعادة الإنضباط ، لتوحيد القيادة), (تشكيل حكومة جديدة ، حل البرلمان ، فرض حالة الطواريء), (الأجهزة الأمنية والعسكرية), (ضباط في الجيش والشرطة)

The (و) is also used inter-sententially to start a new sentence within the same paragraph:

(وأكد), (ووصفوها بأنها . .), (وأنهم باركوا . .), (وأكد أنه . .), (وقال أنه كان . .)
(وأعلن أن الحزب . .), (ونفى ما تردد . .), إلتزام . .)

Also, it is used at the initial position of each paragraph from the second sentence onwards:

(وأوضح . .), (واستهل . .), (وأجاب . .), and (ونفى . .).

It is also important to note that in Arabic, text-initial sentences are verbal with zero conjunction. In other words, the first sentence of the first paragraph in any text variety starts without the conjunctive element (و) or indeed without any other element of conjunction. From the second paragraph onwards, every initial sentence of each paragraph is expected to start with (و) or other conjunctive elements depending on the type of text (see Chapter Four).

Example 3:

جاء أحمد وزبير وأمل وشريفة وأطفالهم ليقضوا العيد معنا – Ahmad, Zubair, Amal, Sharifah, and their children came to spend the Eid with us.

Example 4:

أنها بالتأكيد من صنع خالق حكيم وعليم وقادر ورحيم – They are indeed the make of a wise, aware, able, and most merciful Creator.

In examples 3 and 4, we can notice the recurrent use of the conjunctive (و) among the nouns and adjectives.

Example 5:

وهذا قول يشق على القاريء فهمه ، هذا من جهة ، ومن جهة أُخرى ، فيه خروج عن طبيعة البلاغة التي تتفق مع فطرة النفس

This statement is very difficult for the reader to understand, on the one hand, and it entails a departure from the essence of rhetoric that is compatible with instinct.

Example 6:

ومن جانبه صرح أبتي بطلوف أن القصف الروسي المتواصل أصبح سبباً لمجاعة حقيقية تهدد سكان جنوب الشيشان .

On his part, Abty Batlof stated that the continuous Russian shelling became the reason behind a true famine threatening the population of southern Chechnya.

Example 7:

ومن جهته أعلن رئيس وزراء جمهورية إيرلندة بيرتي أهيرون "نحن هنا من أجل أن نبذل كل ما بوسعنا لتحسين الحياة في هذه الجزيرة في ظل جو من الصداقة"

On his part, the Prime Minister of the Republic of Ireland Mr Bertie Aherne announced that "we are here to do our best to improve the living in this island in an atmosphere of friendship".

Example 8:

جدير بالذكر أن حالة الطواريء في الجزائر سارية المفعول منذ يوم ٨ فبراير (شباط) ١٩٩٢

It is worth mentioning that the state of emergency in Algeria has been in force since 8 February 1992.

Example 9:

وبطبيعة الحال ، فهذه ليست المرة الأولى التي تحاول فيها الدول الغنية التأثير على قرارات الدول المنتجة للنفط

Actually, this is not the first time the rich countries try to influence the decisions of the oil producing countries.

3.3.4.2 Adversative Conjunction الربط الإستدراكي

Adversative conjunction refers to the contradiction relationship between what has been said and what is to come. The typical Arabic adversative conjunctive elements are (لكن ، بيـــــد أنّ - but, however, yet). Other adversative conjunctive elements can be employed for a variety of functions: They can be used for an emphatic effect when we compare different situations or events such as (على نقيض ذلك - on the contrary, by contrast).

Other elements such as (مع ذلك ، بالرغم من ذلك - nevertheless, in spite of this, في الوقت نفسه / في نفس الوقت - at the same time, مع أنَّ ، رغم أنَّ - although, ومن جهة أخري - on the other hand) can also be used for emphatic effect. For an avowal, i.e., when making an open declaration, Arabic uses the adversative conjunctive elements like (في الحقيقة ، في الواقع - in fact, as a matter of fact). When an idea is rejected, adversative conjunctive elements like (على أيَّة حال - anyhow, in any case) can be used.

Example 1:

ومع ذلك فأنه لو تحقق هذا التصعيد فإنَّ ذلك سوف يتيح للولايات المتحدة فرصة التدخل العسكري في المنطقة .

Nevertheless, if this escalation takes place, it will give the United States the opportunity for military intervention in the region.

Example 2:

ورغم أن احتمالات التصعيد واردة إلا أنه لابد وأن يؤثر على العلاقات الأمريكية السوفيتية .

Although the possibility of escalation is likely, this will affect the American-Soviet relations.

Example 3:

في الحقيقة أن هذه المسألة حسَّاسة للغاية – As a matter of fact, this matter is extremely sensitive.

Example 4:

على أيَّة حال هذا الأمر لا يهمُّني – Anyway, this matter is not my concern.

Example 5:

حذَّرته عدَّة مرَّات لكنه لا يبالي – I warned him many times but he did not care

Example 6:

ولكن هناك من يقول أن سياسة بريطانيا الخارجية كانت تسير على خط واحد مع السياسة الأمريكية .

But there are those who say that the British foreign policy was moving on the same line of the American foreign policy.

Example 7:

ومن جهة أخرى كانت السيدة غلوريا فالي قد عثرت في أوكلاهوما وضواحيها على العديد من النقوش المهمة التي تركها ليبيون .

On the other hand, Mrs Gloria Farly has found in Oklahoma and its suburbs many important inscriptions which the Libyans left.

3.3.4.3 Causal Conjunction الربط السَّببي

Causal conjunction refers to the relationship between two sentences in which something or some event is the cause of the other. Usually what is mentioned first is the cause and what is mentioned after is the direct consequence of that cause. The typical Arabic causal conjunctive elements are (لهذا - so, therefore, لأن - because , جراء ، بسبب - because of, إذاً - thus, therefore) which can be used for an emphatic effect. The causal conjunctive elements (فـ ، حيث / إذ - for , since, because) are employed to emphatically substantiate the previous statement. When the reason or purpose is specific, causal conjunctive elements like (نتيجة لذلك ، لهذا الغرض ، لهذا السبب - for this reason, consequently, وبالتالي - thus, ولذا - therefore) can be used. The causal conjunctive element (وإلاّ - otherwise) can be used when the direct cause or condition is known to the hearer. The causal conjunctive element (وهكذا - thus) can be used in the conclusion of an argumentative text to affirm a thesis.

Example 1:
الهواء ضروري فلولاه (إذ لولاه) لما عاش الإنسان – Air is essential for without it Man would not be able to survive.

Example 2:
ياسر أستاذي العزيز إذ لولاه (فلولاه) لما تعلمت هذه الأمور المفيدة – Yasir is my dear teacher for without him I will not be able to learn these useful things.

Example 3:
إسرع وإلا فاتك القطار – Hurry up otherwise you'll miss the train.

Example 4:
ولذا يصح القول بأنّ إستمرار الحرب قد أصبح هدفاً – Therefore, it is right to claim that the continuation of war has become an objective.

Example 5:
وهكذا تتشابك علاقات الدول العظمى مع حرب الخليج – Thus, the relations of the superpowers entangle with the Gulf war.

3.3.4.4 Temporal Conjunction الربط الزّمني

Temporal conjunction refers to the time sequence relationship between sentences. Typical Arabic temporal conjunctive elements are like (ثُمَّ ، ومنْ ثَمَّ ، فـ ، بعد ذلك - then, next, بعد - after, قبل - before) which are used when there is a sequence of events.When there is a simultaneous time sequence, we can use elements like (في نفس الوقت ، في الوقت نفسه - at the same time, أثناء ، بينما - while, في هذا الأثناء ، في غضون ذلك ، ما دام - meanwhile, خلال ، - during, في حينها - at that time, في غضون ذلك - in the meantime). When there is no more time sequence and a conclusion is to be provided, we use temporal conjunctive elements like (أخيراً - finally, وفي الختام ، ختاماً - in conclusion, finally, خُلاصة الأمر ، خلاصة القول ، باختصار - to sum up, briefly). When we list a number of temporal sequences, we can use temporal conjunctive elements like (أولاً - first, firstly, ثانياً - second, secondly, ثالثاً - third, thirdly). Other Arabic temporal conjunctive elements are like (آنذاك - then, at that time, منذ - since, كلما ، متى ما - whenever, من الآن فصاعداً - henceforth, from now on, لحد الآن - up to now, سابقاً - previously).

Example 1:
أرجو من الآن فصاعداً أن تعتمد على نفسك – From now on, please rely on yourself.

Example 2:
لم أسمع منها أي شيء لحد الآن – Up to now, I have not heard anything from her.

Example 3:
وفي الختام ، أتمنى لكم أُمسية سعيدة – Finally, I wish you a happy evening.

Example 4:
باختصار ، هذا الأمر بينك وبينها – In brief, this matter is between you and her.

Example 5:
وخلاصة القول إن إمكانيات التوسُّع الزراعي ضيقة – In brief, the potential for agricultural expansion is limited.

Example 6:
ومضى الى الباب فطرقه ثم دفعه ودخل تتبعه أخته – He went to the door, knocked at it, then pushed it, and went in followed by his sister.

Example 7:
في غضون ذلك هاجم الأمين العام للأمم المتحدة موسكو – In the meantime, the UN General Secretary attacked Moscow.

Example 8:
ختاماً ، أكد البرفسور باري فيل بأن المستوطنين الليبيين قد أدخلوا الطراز الفني الأفريقي واللغات الأفريقية الى أمريكا الشمالية .
Finally, Professor Barry Phil confirmed that the Libyan settlers had introduced the African artistic model and the African languages to North America.

3.3.5 Lexical Cohesion تماسُك العلاقات المُفرداتيّة

Within each text, there are lexical relations that play a significant role in the realization of cohesion from a lexical perspective. Lexical items have a cohesive function. The particular selection of words produces a cohesive impact on the sentence, in particular, and on the text, in general. Lexical cohesion can be realized through the lexical relations of collocation and reiteration.

3.3.5.1 Collocation المُصاحبة اللّفظيّة

Lexical cohesion can be achieved through a mutually exclusive pair of words which are opposites, such as (رجال - men . . . نساء - women), words which belong to the same semantic field, i.e., they share the same lexical environment, like (أكل - to eat . . . مطعم - restaurant, وجبة طعام - a meal; سفارة - embassy . . . جواز - passport, مُلحق - attache) (see 2.2 Semantic Fields), words which have part to whole relationship such as (سيّارة - car . . . إطار - wheel; بيت - house . . . غرفة جلوس - sitting room, حمّام - bathroom), words which have part to part relationship such as (إصبع - finger . . . يد - hand . . . قدم - foot), pairs of words which belong to a set of series such as week days (الإثنين - Monday, جمعة - Friday), calendar months (رمضان , شعبان , تموز/يوليو - July), the four seasons (شتاء - winter, صيف - summer), directions (شمال ، جنوب), army ranks (نقيب - captain, ملازم - lieutenant), currency units (فلس . . . درهم . . . دينار), names of different currencies (دينار ، ريال ، جنيه ، مارك), and words which are cohyponyms of the same superordinate word like (كرسي - chair . . . طاولة - table). All such words have a cohesive effect and are employed for textual purposes (see 2.8 Word Set).

3.3.5.2 Reiteration التكرار

Reiteration, which is a form of lexical cohesion, can be achieved by a number of semantic relations such as the repetition of the same word or phrase, synonymy, near synonymy, superordinate, personal reference forms, and general words. Therefore, reiteration is anaphoric. It is employed in

Arabic to produce a cohesive effect.

Example 1:

إسمعني رجاءاً يامحمود . أُحب لكَ الخير وأُريد أن أنصحك . إنَّ صحتك وعائلتك أهم بكثير من أموالك وأعمالك التجارية فلا تنشغل بها كثيراً وتنسى صحتك وعائلتك . فمن سينفعك يا محمود إذا تدهورت صحتك وتفككت عائلتك ؟ أموالك وأعمالك التجارية ليست كل شيء . هذه نصيحة أخوية وأنتَ حُر .

Mahmood, please listen to me. I wish you good and I want to advise you. Your health and family are more important than your money. You should not be too busy with your business and forget about your health and family. Mahmood, who will benefit you when your health deteriorates and your family breaks up? Your money and your business are not everything. This is brotherly advice and you are free.

Example 2:

الصحة ! ما هي الصحة ؟ هي كمال التوازن والتوافق والتعاون في الكائن ، ولكن هيهات ان تتحقق اذا كانت الصحة العامة معتلة ، خذ مثلا صحة الوزارة ! . .

(نجيب محفوظ - دنيا الله : ١٩٧٢ ص ٢٠٤)

Health! What is health? It is the balance, conformity, and cooperation in the creature. But it can never be achieved if the public health is poor. Take for instance the health of the ministry! . . .

Example 3:

دخلت إلى شقَّته وتفاجئتُ بفقرِه فلم أرى سوى كرسياً واحداً وسريره وهذا كل ما يملك من أثاث .

I entered his flat and I was surprised by his poverty. I only saw a chair and his bed. That was all his furniture.

Example 4:

أخيراً إلتقيت بالرجل الذي إتصل بي يوم أمس وأخبرني بظروفه العائلية . هو طالب جديد ذو ظروف فريدة من نوعها مما جعلني أحس بأن إنساناً كهذا سيكون من الطلبة المتميزين .

In the end, I met the man who contacted me yesterday and told me about his family circumstances. He is a new student with unique circumstances which made me feel that a man like this would be one of the distinguished students.

Example 5:

أعلنت الحكومة الجزائرية أمس الأول أنها ستمدد مُهلة العفو للمجموعات الإسلامية المسلحة لتسليم أنفسهم وأسلحتهم . وأكد متحدث بأسم وزارة الداخلية أن هذا القرار لا علاقة له بزيارة وزير الخارجية الفرنسي إلى الجزائر . . .

The Algerian government announced the day before yesterday that it will extend the grace period of amnesty for the Islamic armed groups to give themselves up and hand in their weapons. A spokesman of the Ministry of Internal Affairs confirmed that this decision had nothing to do with the visit by the French Foreign Minister to Algeria . ... .

In the above examples, we have seen how one word or phrase refers back (anaphoric) to another word or phrase in order to achieve lexical cohesion. In example 1, the reiterated words (محمود - Mahmood, نصيحة - advice) are repetitions of the words (أنصح - to advise, محمود - Mahmood); similarly, the phrases (صحتك - your health, عائلتك - your family, أموالك - your money, أعمالك التجارية - your business) are repetitions of the phrases (صحتك - your health, عائلتك - your family, أموالك - your money, أعمالك التجارية - your business). In example 2, the reiterated words (الصحة ، الصحة ، صحة) are repetitions of the word (الصحة). In example 3, the reiterated words (كرسي - chair, سرير - bed) are the co-hyponyms of the word (أثاث - furniture). In example 4, the reiterated words (هو - he, هذا - this) are personal and demonstrative reference forms respectively of the word (الرجل - the man). In example 5, the reiterated word (القرار - decision) is a general word which represents a group of words (ستمدد مهلة العفو للمجموعات الإسلامية المسلحة لتسليم أنفسهم واسلحتهم).

3.4 Thematic Structure هيكلُ الجُملة ذات المُحدَّث عنه

Thematic structure means the organization of the sentence in terms of its information which it conveys to us as readers or listeners. Lexical elements are placed sentence-initially when they are given importance by the writer/speaker. There is always a good reason for placing an element sentence-initially. The sentence as a message usually contains, within its context, known (old) information and unknown (new) information to the reader/listener. The initial lexical element in a sentence is usually referred to as the Theme of the sentence which can be a verb in the case of basic transitive/intransitive structures (see 1.2.1), or a noun (phrase) in the case of derived sentences (see 1.4). The rest of the sentence is usually referred to as the Rheme. The Theme provides known information when it is mentioned already in the context while the Rheme (the rest of the sentence) provides unknown information. If it is not mentioned in the context before, the Theme becomes unknown to the reader/listener and therefore provides unknown information to us. In basic transitive/intransitive sentences, the initial verb is the unmarked Theme because it is a more frequent word order and there is no good reason for it to be otherwise, as in:

Example 1:

وقبل أن يأكل الأطفال طعامهم طلبت منهم أمهم أن يغسلوا أيديهم ويجلسوا على المائدة بهدوء . جلس سالم الى جنب أمه . أكل طعامه دون أن ينطق كلمة واحدة . ترك المائدة دون أن يستأذن من أمه ...

And before the children ate their food, their mother asked them to wash their hands and sit on the table quietly. Salim sat next to his mother. He ate his food without saying a word. He left the table without asking his mother's permission

In this example, the verbs (جلس - sat) and (أكل - ate) are the unmarked Themes which provide known information because the verbs have been mentioned before in the text. The rest of the two sentences (سالم الى جنب أمه) and (طعامه دون أن ينطق بكلمة واحدة) are the Rhemes. However, the verb (ترك - left) is also an unmarked Theme but it provides unknown information to us because it is not mentioned before.

In derived sentences where the initial element is a noun (phrase), the initial element is the marked Theme because there is good reason to front it such as repeating it because it was mentioned before or contrasting it. The marked Theme in derived sentences can also provide either known or unknown information, as in:

Example 2:

إنَّ إستمرار الحرب قد أصبح هدفاً في ذاته . ولذا فان الولايات المتحدة لا تجد في استمرار الحرب خطراً يدفعها الى العمل على إعادة السلام . وروسيا تنظر الى الحرب نظرة مختلفة عن النظرة الأمريكية . . . وروسيا تحقق إكتفاءاً ذاتياً من النفط . . . وروسيا ليست صاحب مصلحة في إستمرار الحرب .

The continuity of the war became an objective in itself. Therefore, the United States does not find in the continuity of the war a danger that forces her to work for the restoration of peace. Russia looks at the war differently from America. Russia is self-sufficient in oil. Russia does not have any interest in the continuity of the war.

In this example, the sentence-initial noun phrase (إستمرار الحرب - the continuity of war) is the marked Theme which provides unknown information to us. The noun phrase (الولايات المتحدة - the United States) is also a marked Theme which provides unknown information. Also, we have the sentence-initial noun (روسيا - Russia) as the marked Theme which provides unknown information in the first instance only while when it is repeated again, it provides known information.

Note that the initial particles like (إنَّ) and (لذا فإن) are not taken into consideration because they are not part of the sentence structure. The same applies to adjuncts which are quite mobile; they also should not be called Themes because they are not at the heart of the sentence structure; they are just added on.

Practical Exercises

تطبيقات

1. Underline the words which contribute in the realization of lexical cohesion and mention their cohesive function:

١. ويعتبر النحل من أذكى الحشرات وأنفعها للإنسان فلولاها لما ذقنا العسل وعرفناه بأنواعه المختلفة . وتعتمد نوعية العسل على نوعية الزهور التي يزورها النحل .

٢. – وأنا ألا تريد أن أعدكَ بشيء ؟

– أريد . . أريد بكل تأكيد . .

– ولماذا تريد أنتَ . . ولا أريد أنا ؟ !

٣. ما هي الدوافع ؟ لا أدري . . ولكني لم أعد أشعر بحاجتي الى لقائه . . وكنت في هذه الوحدة التي تركتني فيها أبي . .لا أنام . . أطوف بين الغرف كأني أهرب من غرفة الى غرفة ، وأحس في هربي بطنط صفية تلاحقني . . أكاد أرى صورتها على الجدران ، وأكاد أحس بأنفاسها خلف أذني ، وأكاد أسمع خطواتها تتبع خطواتي . . أنها في كل مكان من البيت . . كانت تجلس هنا . . وكانت تأكل هنا . . وهنا كانت تقف لمراقبة الخدم . . وهنا كانت تشغل التريكو . . وهنا . . وهنا . . وهنا . .

٤. سيخرج من السجن كل من لا يستحق السجن حقاً ولو فرغت السجون !

٥. غادر القهوة ليسير بلا هدف على ما في ذلك من جهد لم يعتده . ووجد نفسه يمر بسينما فدخل . ولم يلبث فيها إلا نصف ساعة ثم غادرها وهو يزفر مللاً ويأساً . وعاد الى البيت ذليلاً . . أما حفل التكريم هذا فهو آخر ما يربطه بالماضي . وهو حدث له أهميته .

2. Provide complete sentences as examples for:

(i) cohesion through personal reference

(ii) cataphoric reference

(iii) anaphoric reference

(iv) nominal substitution

(v) verbal substitution

(vi) verbal ellipsis

(vii) nominal ellipsis

(viii) lexical cohesion through reiteration

(ix) lexical cohesion through collocation

3. Provide sentences with the conjunctive elements (أذ), (فـ), and (ثم).
4. Provide sentences with the conjunctive elements (على صعيد آخر) and (ومن جهة أخرى).
5. What does the conjunctive element (إذ) substantiate in the following sentence?

ولم يكد يمضي إسبوعان حتى وقع حادث لايقل غرابة عن سابقه ، إذ سقط جسم من آخر عربة للترام رقم ٣٣ شارع عشرة آخر الليل .
(نجيب محفوظ – دنيا الله ١٩٧٢ ص ١١١)

6. Underline anaphoric and cataphoric reference and its referent in the following sentences:

١. ولابُدَّ من موافقة الكونغرس الأمريكي على الصفقة قبل تنفيذها . وفي حال إتمامها ستكون دولة الإمارات الدولة الأولي خارج دول حلف الأطلسي التي تحصل على هذا الطراز المتطور من الطائرات العسكرية الأمريكية .
(جريدة الرياض : ص ٣٨ الإثنين ٦ مارس ٢٠٠٠)

٢. ومن جانبها قالت صحيفة تشرين أن إسلوب المماطلة والتسويف الذي يتبناه الوفد الإسرائيلي المفاوض ولجوء باراك الى المناورة هما السبب الحقيقي وراء توقف المباحثات وتزايد الشكوك في النيات الإسرائيلية .
(جريدة الأهرام : ص ١ الأحد ٣٠ يناير ٢٠٠٠)

٣. وقال أحمد وهو ينظر الى خاله في سخط وكراهية : "طيب . . أودعك" واندفع خارج الغرفة ثم دخل غرفته ، وصفق الباب وراءه . . وهرولت الأم الى أخيها ، وصاحت فيه وهي تنشب عينيها في وجهه كأنها تتهمه بإيذاء ولدها . . ولدها الوحيد . .
(إحسان عبد القدوس – لا تُطفيء الشمس ١٩٦٠ ص ٤٣٢-٤٣١)

٤. بعد تحمله العبء الأكبر في الكفاح ضد الأرهاب ، يتجه الجيش الجزائري خطوة تلو الاخرى نحو الإحتراف .
(العرب ٢٤/٢/٢٠٠٠ ص ١)

7. Underline the word that contributes in the cohesion of the following sentences and give the type of cohesion it performs:

١. أرمي هذه الفاكهة والخضروات واذهب واشتري غيرها .

٢. وذهبتُ فوراً الى عيادة الطبيب وجلست أنتظر دوري ثم جلست جنبي عجوز سرعان ما بادرتني بسؤالها : "ما بكَ ؟" . فأجبت ببرود : "أشكو من الصُداع والبرد . وأنتِ ؟"
– أنا كذلك

8. Explain the stylistic impact of the causal conjunctive cohesive elements (إذ) and (فـ) and their semantic meaning in the following sentences:

١. كان العسكريون لا يؤمنون بقدرة الأحزاب على القيام بهذه المهمة إذ أنَّ الأحزاب هي جزء من مشكلة مصر .
(ناجي علوش – الثورة والجماهير ١٩٦٢ ص ٢٥٠)

٢. تُعتبر الأحياء الدقيقة من المصادر الجيدة لبعض الفيتامينات . فالخميرة مثلاً تُعد من أغنى المصادر المعروفة في فيتامينات المجموعة ب ، وخصوصاً الفيتامين ب ١ . أما الطحالب فتحتوي الى جانب فيتامينات ب كميات كبيرة من مولد فيتامين E.
(مجلة العربي : ص ١١٥ العدد ١٨٥ أبريل (نيسان) ١٩٧٤)

9. Use the conjunctive elements (ومن الطريف أنَّ ، من ناحية أخرى ، وفي الوقت نفسه ، من جانبه ، بيد أنَّ / ولكن ، إذاً ، في الحقيقة ، باختصار ، مع ذلك ، بينما) in sentences.

10. Underline the Theme and identify the type of information it provides in the following texts:

١. السؤال الرئيسي الذي يشغل بال القيادة العسكرية الأمريكية فيما يتعلق بحرب الخليج هو كيفية عدم التورط في حرب طويلة الأمد . وهذا السؤال هو بالذات ما ستركز عليه اللجنة العسكرية الخاصة . فالموضوع من وجهة النظر الأمريكية لم يعد مقتصراً على خفايا وأبعاد هذه الحرب . إذ أن القيادة العسكرية الأمريكية ، وتحديداً القيادة البحرية ، لايمكن أن تنظر بعين الرضى الى ما يجري في هذه المنطقة الحسَّاسة .
(الشرق الأوسط : ١٩٨٨/٧/٦ ص ٢)

٢. لقد بدأنا معركة التحرير في ٢٣ يوليو سنة ١٩٥٢ ، وكانت مصر نهباً لفئة قليلة من الناس . إن لكل منا شكاية وكلنا مظلومون . لقد قمنا بهذه الثورة حتى نتَّحد مع الشعب ، ولقد استطعنا في عام أنْ نتحرر من التقاليد والعقائد والعادات التي أضرَّت بنا . يجب أنْ نعرف حقوقنا أولاً . ولا أجد مثلاً لهذا أقرب من الإنتخابات . لقد كان الظلم يتفشى بيننا . لقد مكَّنا نحن للظلم أنْ ينجح في هذه البلاد بضعفنا وتهاوننا . والآن وقد تحررنا من ظلم الحكام علينا ان نتحرر من ظلم أنفسنا . لقد تحررنا من الظلم السياسي ولكن هل تحررنا من الظلم الإجتماعي ؟ أننا لم نتحرر من الظلم الإجتماعي . فإن آثار الماضي مازالت تطغي علينا .
(خُطب وتصريحات الرئيس جمال عبد الناصر / الجزء الأول – ١٩٩٥ ص ١٠٢)

٣. الصياد : إنك أيها الجني لست إنسي حتى تعرف حقيقة القلب الانساني .
الجني : قلت لكَ إسكت أنتَ بجهلكَ وغبائكَ . القلب الانساني حقيقته أبسط من أي حقيقة .
(توفيق الحكيم – سليمان الحكيم : ١٩٥٧ ص ١٠١)

٤. الخمائر : ومنها أجناس تُربى على بيئات تحتوي على السكر . والخمائر نجدها

منذ القدم في كثير من أطعمتنا .
(مجلة العربي : العدد ١٨٥ أبريل (نيسان) ١٩٧٤ ص ١١٥)

٥. لكل شيء دواء أيها الملك . إصغوا إليَّ . إصغوا إليَّ . لكل شيء دواء إلاَّ اليأس . اليأسُ وحده هو البلاءُ الذي لايوجد له دواء .
(توفيق الحكيم – سليمان الحكيم : ١٩٥٧ ص ٩٧)

٦. الملك : عندي إذاً حسن تدبير وسلامة تفكير .
الوزير : بدون شك يامولاي .
الملك : قل هذا لجلالة الملكة !
الملكة : جلالة الملكة يهمها النتائج العملية قبل كل شيء .
(توفيق الحكيم – مصير صرصار : ١٩٧٧ ص ٢٣)

٧. – هل تقتل الحاج عبدالصمد ؟
– أقتل ! القتلُ شيءٌ لم أجربه !
(نجيب محفوظ – دنيا الله : ١٩٧٢ ص ٨٥)

٨. أطفالنا وشاشة التلفاز
أطفالنا هم الهدف المكشوف الذي تتساقط عليه سهام الشاشة الصغيرة بلا رحمة ولا فتور .
(مجلة الوعي الاسلامي : تموز – آب ١٩٩٦ ص ٥)

11. Underline the words that take part in the lexical cohesion in the following text and identify each type:

خرجنا الى الصيد في الغابة ومعنا كلاب الصيد ورأت الكلاب ثعلباً فطاردته وأخذت تعدو وراءه عدواً سريعاً . دار الثعلب دورة واسعة والكلاب من خلفه . وتكررت المطاردة مرَّات ، حتى تعبت الكلاب ، وظهر عليها الإرهاق والجهد . تعجب الصيادون وقال واحد منهم : كيف تتعب الكلاب الى هذا الحد والثعلب نشيط لم يتعب ؟
(المفتاح للقراءة والكتابة / للسنة الثانية ، سلطنة عُمان / وزارة التربية والتعليم والشباب : ١٩٩٠ ص ٩٦)

Chapter Four
Text Types in Arabic
أنواعُ النُّصوصِ العربيَّة

4.1 Introduction

We use texts to communicate with each other. Texts vary in the length of their linguistic sequences. The building elements of these texts are words and sentences which have mutual dependence and do not occur at random. Texts also contain a number of paragraphs which are anaphoric to each other, i.e., they refer coherently to each other. A text, however, may contain one paragraph only, just like a text of one word or one sentence. The paragraph is a text unit that also enjoys texture and which is bigger in size than the sentence. However, it is not an independent unit as it is tied up to other paragraphs which all combine to form a whole coherent and cohesive text. An important feature of Arabic texts is that they prototypically contain long paragraphs, lacking in punctuation as it is not an inherent linguistic norm of Arabic. To the learner of Arabic, this makes the sentence look long. Each text hangs together by means of texture and represents a coherent whole. Texts are context-bound, i.e., each text type is produced for and conditioned by a specific context. Therefore, we come across a variety of Arabic text types each of which is for a particular context and is characterized by special linguistic features. Each text type enjoys its own stylistic hallmarks. The major Arabic text types are journalistic, advertisement, scientific, narrative, letter, poetry, instructional, descriptive, expository and argumentative.

4.2 Arabic Text Types أنواع النصوص العربية

4.2.1 News Reports تقارير الأخبار

These are basic journalistic texts (النصوص الصحفية) that are used in the media. The language of journalism is clear and simple because newspapers are usually read in a hurry. The news report is meant to be informative but not in a complicated language. As a direct influence of European journalistic style, the hallmarks of Arabic journalistic text are the use of short paragraphs compared to medieval Arabic style, the use of subject-initial sentences especially in headlines and captions, the use of cataphoric reference, frequent use of cliches, use of loan words for glamorous appeal like (ستراتيجية - strategy, أكاديمية - academy, تكتيك - tactics, آيديولوجية - ideology, idea, دراماتيكي - dramatic), non-traditional punctuation especially the use of the comma, and occasional grammatical errors especially in the use of prepositions. The main characteristic features of an Arabic journalistic text include the use of special ad hoc cohesive conjunctive ties at the beginning of each paragraph except for the first paragraph. The prototypical journalistic conjunctive elements are like (على صعيد آخر - on the other hand; من جهة أخرى - on the other hand; من جهته - on his part), the use of special verbs like (أكد - to stress, confirm; أضاف قائلاً / وأضاف - to add saying; قال - to say; صرح - to announce) which are preceded by the conjunctive (و - and). We also find the recurrent use of the additive conjunctive element (و) at the beginning of most paragraphs except for the first one and the occasional use of fronted adjuncts. The news report has a headline. It sometimes has a main headline and a sub-headline. Main and sub-headlines are usually nominal sentences, i.e., they start with a noun phrase. Sometimes, we encounter long headlines and some of which include quotations, as in:

الرئيس اليمني : أمريكا تتوسط لحل نزاع الحدود مع السعودية وتعارض القمة العربية ... وأنصح الرئيس صدام بالمرونة والصبر
(صحيفة القدس العربي : ص١ الأربعاء ٢٣ شباط (فبراير) ٢٠٠٠)

The Yemeni President: America mediates to solve the border dispute with Saudi Arabia and opposes the Arab summit ... and I advise President Saddam to be flexible and patient.

أولبرايت : الخيار العسكري يشجع المتطرفين في القوقاز
(الحياة : ص١ الخميس ٣ شباط (فبراير) ٢٠٠٠)

Albright: The military option encourages the extremists in the Caucasus

The first paragraph of the journalistic text starts with a verbal sentence (verb-initial sentence) without any cohesive tie, i.e., without any conjunctive element before the verb. Other paragraphs also start with a verbal sentence but usually the conjunctive element (و) is used before the verb and sometimes other ad hoc journalistic cohesive elements are used paragraph-initially before the verb. Before the start of the first paragraph, however, we find the name of the city from which the news report is written or issued followed by either the abbreviation of the news agency or the name of the news reporter. Arabic journalistic texts also contain quotations, i.e., direct speech put inside inverted commas. These are statements of an official, spokesman, head of state, an ordinary person, etc., that are mentioned to provide credibility to the news report. We also find(قـــــام . . بـــ ، تم) constructions, double adjectives like (الخلاف القطري البحريني), calques and loan words (see 2.26 and 2.27).

Example 1:

وزيرا خارجية قطر والبحرين يؤكدان النية الصادقة لحل نزاع الحدود " أخوياً"

المنامة – أف ب : أكد وزيرا خارجية البحرين وقطر الشيخ محمد مبارك آل خليفة والشيخ حمد بن جاسم آل ثاني على وجود "نية صادقة لدى البلدين للخروج بحل أخوي" للخلاف الحدودي بينهما الذي كان مدار بحث في إجتماعات الدورة الأولى للَّجنة العليا بين البلدين .

وقال وزير الخارجية البحريني خلال مؤتمر صحافي مشترك الإثنين مع نظيره القطري حول نتائج هذه الإجتماعات "أن الخلاف الحدودي بين البحرين وقطر تم بحثه في إجتماع الدورة الأولى للجنة العليا المشتركة بين البلدين" .

وأوضح أن "الجانبين إتفقا على أنْ يُستكمل بحث هذا الموضوع في إجتماعات قادمة".

وأضاف أنه تم خلال الإجتماع "التوقيع على الإتفاقية التي تقضي بإنشاء اللجنة العُليا البحرينية القطرية المشتركة لتصبح في إطارها القانوني الصحيح".

أما وزير الخارجية القطري فأشار من جهته إلى أن "الخلاف القطري البحريني يُنظرُ فيه حالياً في محكمة العدل الدولية".

وقال أن "موضوع الخلاف بين البحرين وقطر يُناقَشُ في جو هاديء وبعيداً عن الأضواء بحيث أننا نهدف مِنْ خلال ذلك إلى نتيجة".

ويُذكر أنَّ محكمة العدل الدوَلية ستبدأ في ٢٩ أيار (مايو) المُقبل ببحث هذا الخلاف الذي رفعته إليها قطر في العام ١٩٩١ مِنْ طرف واحد .

وحول ما إذا كان قرار محكمة العدل الدولية سيُعرقل مسيرة العلاقات الثنائية بين البلدين ، أوضح وزير الخارجية القطري أن "التوَجُّه الودي لن يعرقله قرار المحكمة كما ورد في بيان المنامة".

وأكَّد "إحترام دولة قطر لقرار المحكمة الذي سيصدر في حال عدم التوصل إلى حل أخوي".

ومِنْ جهة أُخرى ورداً على سؤال حول العلاقات البحرينية الإسرائيلية ، قال وزير الخَارجية البحريني أن "سياسة دولة البحرين تجاه هذا الموضوع تنبع مِنْ قرارات مجلس التعاون لدول الخليج العربية" مُؤكداً أن "سياسة مجلس التعاون في هذا الإطار واضحة وهي تأييد ودفع عملية السلام في الشرق الأوسط".

وأشار إلى أن "التطبيع يتمُّ حسب خطوات التقدم في هذا التوجه".

وأوضح أن "اللَّجنة إستعرضت أيضاً عدداً مِن القضايا والمواضيع التي تهم وتعزز وتدعم العلاقات بين البلدين".

وأضاف أن "الجانبين قررا أيضاً السماح لمواطني البلدين التنقل بالبطاقة الشخصية".

(القدس العربي : ص٣ الأربعاء ٢٣ شباط (فبراير) ٢٠٠٠)

The Foreign Ministers of Qatar and Bahrain Affirm Their Genuine Intention to Solve the Border Dispute in a "Brotherly" Way

Manama - AFB

The Foreign Ministers of Qatar and Bahrain, Sheikh Muhammad Mubarak Al Khalifah and Sheikh Hamad bin Jasim Al Thani, confirmed the existence of a "genuine intention from both countries to reach a brotherly solution" for the border dispute between them which was the main theme of the first session of talks of the supreme committee between the two countries.

Talking about the results of these meetings, the Foreign Minister of Bahrain said on Monday during a joint press conference with his counterpart, the Foreign Minister of Qatar, that "the border dispute between Bahrain and Qatar has been discussed in the first session of the joint supreme committee between the two countries" and also explained that "the two sides have agreed that the discussion of this matter be completed in future meetings."

"The agreement which demands the establishment of a joint Bahrain-Qatari supreme committee has been signed during the meeting to be within its right legal frame", he added.

The Foreign Minister of Qatar, on his part, said that "the dispute between Qatar and Bahrain is being considered by the International Court of Justice". He said "the dispute between Bahrain and Qatar is being discussed in a quiet atmosphere far away from the spotlights because we aim at achieving a result from that".

The International Court of Justice will start next May 29 investigating this dispute which was forwarded unilaterally by Qatar in 1991.

On whether the decision by the International Court of Justice may obstruct the progress of the bilateral relations between the two countries, the Foreign Minister of Qatar explained that "the friendly attitude will not be hampered by the International Court of Justice decision as it has been referred to in the Manama statement" and confirmed that "Qatar respects the decision of the Court which will be taken in case a brotherly solution is not achieved".

In his response to the question on the Bahraini-Israeli relations, the Foreign Minister of Bahrain said that "the policy of Bahrain on this matter stems from the Gulf Co-operation Council's decision" and confirmed that "the GCC's

policy in this regard is clear which is support for and pushing forward the Middle East peace process." He also stated that "the normalization is taking place according to the steps of progress in this regard."
He explained that "the Committee also reviewed a number of matters and topics which benefit and support the relations between the two countries." "The two sides also decided to allow the citizens of the two countries to travel with their identity cards", he added.

Example 2:

برعاية "المؤتمر الإسلامي" وحضور ممثل الأُمم المتحدة
محادثات منفصلة في جدّة اليوم بين فرقاء النزاع في أفغانستان
الرياض – عبدالله الطلحة – رويترز :
قال مسؤولون في منظمة المؤتمر الإسلامي أمس أن الفصائل الأفغانية المتحاربة ستحضر محادثات للسلام تستضيفها المنظمة في مقرها بجدة .
وأضافوا أن مجموعة الإتصال التابعة للمنظمة ستبدأ المحادثات بإجتماعات منفصلة اليوم مع ممثلين من حركة (طالبان) الحاكمة ومن المعارضة على أن تُعقد إجتماعات مباشرة بين الجانبين في وقت لاحق .
(الرياض : ص ١ الإثنين ٦ مارس ٢٠٠٠)

Under the Auspices of the Islamic Conference Organization and the Attendance of UN Representative
Separate Talks in Jeddah Today Between Afghan Warring Groups
(Riyadh - Abdullah Al-Yalhah - Reuter)
Officials from the Islamic Conference Organization said yesterday that the Afghan warring factions will attend the peace talks hosted by the Organization in its headquarters in Jeddah. They also added that the contact group of the Organization will start today its separate meetings with representatives from the ruling Taliban movement and from the opposition and that direct talks between the two sides will take place later on.

Example 3:

بعد ساعات من إسقاط القوات البحرية الأمريكية في الخليج طائرة ركاب أيرانية ، مما أدى الى مصرع ٢٩٨ شخصاً أصدرت الخارجية الأمريكية أوامرها للسفارات والقواعد العسكرية الأمريكية في شتى أنحاء العالم باتخاذ إجراءات حراسة مشددة .
(الأهرام : ٥ يوليو (تموز) ١٩٨٨ ص ١)

Hours after the shooting down of an Iranian airliner by the American Navy in the Gulf which led to the death of 298 people, the American State Department issued orders to American bases and embassies all over the world to take extra security measures.

4.2.2 Advertisement Text نص الإعلانات

The language of advertisement ((الإعـــلان (الـدعـــايـة)) is persuasive. Advertisement texts are produced to influence the choice of the reader/hearer using special emotive or non-emotive expressions. Exaggerated language is used to make products seem glamorous. Other features of instructional texts are the use of direct (second person) address, including imperatives; often the product name appears as the initial typographical sentence (or unit); use of exclamation marks (unknown in classical Arabic); few subordinate clauses; absolute words like superlatives (الأفضل - the best; الأقل - the least); lexical items like (فقط - just, only; إطلاقاً - absolutely, totally); intensifiers like (جـداً - very) which occur in sentence initial position; ameliorative words like (لطيف - nice; منعش - refreshing). We usually find lexical cohesion through reiteration of the noun (phrase), as in examples one, four and seven. We also find lexical cohesion through synonyms, as in examples one, four and seven where we have (صفات) and (خُصوصية)meaning (features, characteristics), (مُطَهِّر) and (مُعَقِّم) meaning (detergent) and (يُسر) and (سُهولة) meaning (ease). Advertisement texts also contain instructional sentences as part of persuasion, as in example six (جرِّبها - Try it) and example seven (لا تشعر بالندم - Do not feel remorse), (إحصل على - Get them). This type of text also contains special sentence structures which are concise and mostly noun phrases as modifiers of the noun which is the name of the commercial product, as in:

Example 1:

عطر لويفي للرجال
عِطرَ لويفي كلاسيكي في صفاته وحسَّاسيَّته ! عصريٌّ في خُصوصيَّته وتفرُّده !

Loewe, for men. Loewe perfume is classical in its features and sensitivity!
Modern in its specialness and uniqueness !

Example 2:

بي بوب
عِطرِ قَلَبَ كُلَّ الموازين ! للرجُل !

Be Bop
Perfume which has changed all balance! For men!

Example 3:

ديتول
مُنتج جديد للعناية الشخصية . لَكِ ولجميع أفراد عائلتِكِ .

Dettol

A new product for personal care. For you (fs) and for all members of your family.

Example 4:

ديتول
المُطَهِّر الجديد
ديتول
المُعَقِّم للعناية الجديدة
لأنك تحرِصين على توفيرِ العناية الكاملة لنظافة منزِلك ، ولأنك تثقين بديتول وبفاعَليتِه الأكيدة في قتلَ الميكروبات والجراثيم ، لذلكَ فَإنَّ ديتوَل يُقَدِّمُ لكِ اليوم نوعاً جديداً من العناية .
ديتول المُطَهِّر للعناية الشخصية ، مُطَهِّر لطيف ، شفاف اللون ، ذو رائحة جديدة منعشة ، تم تركيبه خصيصاً ليتوافق مع إحتياجات أُسرتكِ الصحية لكل يوم .
يمكنك الوثوق دائماً بديتول . لأنَّ ديتول يحمي .
(المجلة : ص ٥٢ العدد ٦٩٨ في ٢٧ يونيو (حزيران) ٣٠ يوليو (تموز) ١٩٩٣)

Dettol
The new detergent
Dettol
Disinfectant for new care
Because you (fs) are eager to provide total care for the cleanliness of your house, and because you are confident of Dettol and its affirmed effectiveness in killing germs and microbes; therefore Dettol offers you today a new kind of care.
The detergent Dettol for personal care, a nice, translucent Dettol with a new refreshing smell; it has been made specially to meet your family's everyday hygienic needs. You can always trust Dettol because Dettol protects.

Example 5:

هاي لايت
جودة يابانية
نكهة أمريكية

hi-lite
Japanese excellence.
American flavour.

Example 6:

ميريت ١ الجديدة – جرِّبها
النكهة الأفضل إطلاقاً بالقطران الأقل

The new Merit 1. Try it.

The best flavour at all with the least nicotine.

As part of the persuasive techniques adopted in an advertisement text, we find the use of the assertive particle (أنَّ / إنَّ - verily, indeed) to assert the topic of the text, the emphatic negative particle (لن - will never), lexical items like (فقط - just, only; إطلاقاً - absolutely, totally), exaggeration phrases like (ليلاً أو نهاراً day or night; على مدار الساعة - twenty four hours; بكل يسر وسهولة - easily and with no trouble), or the passive participle (إسمُ المفعول) like (مُرحَّبٌ - they are welcomed by) used also for affirmation, as in:

Example 7:

البنك السعودي الأمريكي
خدمات بنكية عالمية المستوى
الطريقة المثلى لحماية مالك عند السفر
عند حملك شيكات سامبا فيزا السياحية بدلاً من النقد لايمكن أنْ تُترك واقفاً في العراء . لأنك حتى وإنْ فقدتها فإنك لن تخسرها .
عند فقدان شيكات سامبا فيزا السياحية في الخارج ، فقط إتَّصل بسامبا ليلاً أو نهاراً على الهاتف (٥٨١١-٤٠٣-١-٩٦٦) أينما كنت ، وسوف نقوم بإجراء اللاَّزم لتعويضك عن شيكاتك السياحية المفقودة .
إنَّ شيكات سامبا فيزا السياحية مُرَحَّب بها لدى ملايين المؤسَّسات حول العالم .
ويُمكنُك الحصول عليها بكل يُسر وسهولة على مدار الساعة عن طريق أجهزة سامبا للصرف الألكتروني . كما يمكنك الحصول عليها مِن جميع فروعنا في أنحاء المملكة .
لا تشعر بالندم بسبب فقدانك للنقود ، إحصل على شيكات سامبا فيزا السياحية وأنعم براحة البال أينما كنت .
(المجلة : ص ٧٦ العدد ٦٩٨ في ٢٧ يونيو (حزيران) ٣٠ يوليو (تموز) ١٩٩٣)

Saudi American Bank
Bank services at international level
The unique method of protecting your money during travelling
When you carry Samba Visa travellers' cheques instead of cash, you will not be left standing alone in the open because even if you lose them, you have not lost them.
When you lose Samba Visa travellers' cheques abroad, just contact Samba day or night on 966-1-403-5811 wherever you are and we will do the rest to refund you your lost travellers' cheques.
Samba Visa travellers' cheques are welcomed by millions of institutions world wide.
You can get them easily and with no trouble twenty four hours a day through Samba's electronic dispensing cash machines. You can also get them from all

our branches throughout the Kingdom.
Do not feel sorry because you have lost your money. Get Samba Visa travellers' cheques and enjoy peace of mind wherever you are.

Example 8:

للراغبين في الزواج ، البيع ، الشراء ، الكراء
إلى الباحثين عن نصفهم الآخر ، لا تبحثوا كثيراً ولا تسألوا ... فقط إتَّصلوا بالهاتف ١٨٤٠.
جرِّبوا ،
قد تكون اللَّحظة التي تغيِّر مجرى حياتكم
(جريدة الأنوار التونسية : ص ١٦ السبت ٢٩ جانفي الى ٤ فيفري ٢٠٠٠)

For those who want to get married, to sell, to buy, to hire
For those who are looking for their other half. Do not keep looking for too long and do not ask . . . Just contact the telephone number 1840.
Try
It can be the moment that may change the course of your life.

4.2.3 Scientific Text النص العلمي

Scientific and technical texts provide factual information and are usually free from emotive, connotative and figurative expressions. Foreign scientific loan words, however, are used in abundance. The other hallmarks of scientific texts are the use of the conjunctive (و), the employment of reiteration of some lexical items, the use of active and passive participles, and the recurrent use of active sentences.

Example 1:

يعكف علماء بريطانيون على تجارب بدأت في التبلور بشأن الوصول إلى أبقار خالية من الكوليسترول للوقاية من أمراض القلب . وهذه الأبقار ستكون قادرة بسبب نظام غذائي معين على إبعاد مادة الكوليسترول من دمائها ويكون لحم هذه الأبقار والألبان المستخلصة منها خالياً تماماً من هذه المادة .
الألبان والأجبان المستخلصة من الأبقار مادة غنية ومناسبة لبناء الجسم غير أن إكتشاف الكوليسترول وما يسببه من أمراض القلب نبَّه إلى أثر هذه المواد السلبي على الصحة العامة .
وتجري كذلك تجارب تستهدف تهجين بعض الخضروات بمواد إضافية بحيث تكون قادرة على إمتصاص مادة الكوليسترول من الدم وتشكيل حاجز وقاية ضد إنتشارها .
وتظهر في الأسواق البريطانية قريبا خضروات مُكافحة لعناصر الكوليسترول وتمتص خطرها في عملية تهجين واسعة تشرف عليها مراكز الأبحاث في وزارة الزراعة البريطانية .

(المجلة الثقافية : ص٧٦ العدد ٢٤ شوال/ذو القعدة (مارس) ١٤١٨ / ١٩٨٩)

British scientists are currently working on experiments which have begun to take shape to develop cows free from cholesterol to avoid heart diseases. With special diet, these cows will be able to get rid of cholesterol from their blood. The meat and milk taken from these cows will also be completely free from this substance.

Cheese and milk taken from cows are rich materials and suitable for building the body but the discovery of cholesterol and the heart diseases it can cause has warned about the negative effect of these materials on the general health.

There are also other experiments taking place which aim at modifying some vegetables with additional materials so that they become able to absorb the cholesterol from blood and form a protective barrier against its spread.

Shortly, there will be on the British markets vegetables capable of fighting cholesterol and absorbing its danger thanks to an extensive process of genetic modification supervised by the research centre of the British Department of Agriculture.

Example 2:

لقد فرغ علماء الفضاء مُؤقَّتاً من دراسة القمر الذي هو أقرب أجرام السماء إلى الأرض وذهبوا إلى الفضاء الفسيح الذي يليه . وإذا إستعرضنا برنامج "أبولو" الأمريكي الذي إنتهى في ديسمبر ١٩٧٢ ، نجده قد إستهدف دراسة القمر ، وجيولوجيا صخوره ، وطوبغرافية سطحه . وترك رواد الفضاء على سطحه عشرات من الأجهزة العلمية التي سيظل بعضها يعمل لعشرات السنوات المقبلة .
ويمثل مختبر الفضاء "سكاي لاب" بُعداً جديداً في طريق الإنسان إلى الكوكب .
وأقرب الكواكب إلى الأرض هما كوكبا الزهرة والمريخ ، ولا شك أنهما يمثلان محطات الفضاء المقبلة .

إن "سكاي لاب" يُمثل قمة في إنجازات التكنولوجية في عصر الفضاء لذلك يعلق علماء الفضاء أهمية كبرى على تجارب "سكاي لاب" البايولوجية والفسيولوجية وأثر إنعدام الوزن في الرواد إذ سيكون لها آثارها على الرحلات المقبلة في السفر إلى الكواكب . ولا يغيب عن البال أن المؤثرات السايكولوجية على الرواد خلال رحلات "سكاي لاب" الثلاث محل دراسة أيضاً .

(مجلة العربي : ص٣٨ العدد ١٨٥ أبريل (نيسان) ١٩٧٤)

Space scientists have finished for the moment a study of the moon which is the nearest celestial body to Earth and have gone on to the vast space beyond it. If we review the American Apollo programme which ended in December 1972, we will find that it targeted the study of the moon, the geology of its rocks, and the typography of its surface. The American scientists left on its surface tens of scientific instruments some of which will be operational for tens of years to come.

Sky Lab represents a new dimension in Man's road to the planet. The nearest planets to Earth are Mars and Venus. Undoubtedly, they represent the next space stations.

Sky Lab represents the summit of technology in the space age. Therefore, space scientists attach great importance to its biological and physiological experiments as well as the effect of astronauts' loss of gravity. These will have their impact on the next journeys to the planets. It is important to note that the psychological effects on astronauts during the three Sky Lab journeys are also currently under study.

Example 3:

توصّلت أبحاث الشرطة البريطانية إلى إختراع جهاز الكتروني صغير يتولى الإرشاد عن اللصوص ويتولى إعطاء بيانات عن الأماكن السرية التي يحتفظون فيها بالمسروقات المختلفة .

ويمكن وضع هذا الجهاز الصغير جداً داخل سيارات أو دراجات واستقبال الموجات التي يرسلها عبر شاشة خاصة لدى قوات الأمن التي تهاجم أوكار الجريمة وتضبط المجرمين وهم في حالة تلبُّس .

وقد بدأت الشرطة بزرع هذا الجهاز الصغير للغاية في عدة دراجات وتركها بلا حراسة كطُعم يستهدف إستدراج اللصوص إلى السرقة .

(الثقافية : ص٧٧ العدد ٢٤ شوال/ذو القعدة ١٤١٨)

Research by the British police have managed to invent a small electronic system able to direct the police to burglars and give statements about their hide-outs where they keep their stolen goods.

It is possible to put this tiny system inside cars or bicycles and receive the frequencies it sends to a special display of the intelligence police who immediately raid the criminals' hide-outs and catch the criminals red-handed.

The police started to plant this tiny system in a number of bicycles which were left without being guarded in order to be used as baits to attract the thieves to steal them.

4.2.4 Narrative Text النص الروائي

4.2.4.1 Fictional النص القصصي

1. Prose Fiction (القصة): This type of text involves novels, short stories and folktales which are all usually written for silent reading. The narrative convention is characterized by dialogue turns of different lengths and reported speech. The dialogue between characters and their statements are generally fictional. The stylistic hallmark of fictional narrative is the use of

modern standard Arabic. The typical features are the use of the third person, the use of the conjunctive element (و) which connects the narrative sequence, the use of the conjunctive element (فـ) which indicates that each action is a consequence of the previous one, the use of reiteration, emotive, figurative and connotative expressions, presentation, choice of words, use of some colloquial or foreign words, use of idiomatic expressions, synonymy and near synonymy. The descriptive paragraphs of some novels and short stories are also characterized by asyndeton, i.e., lack of cohesive devices especially the additive conjunctive element (و - and).

Example 1:

وخرج من غرفته مندفعاً كالصاروخ المشتعل . . إنه لايريد أن يبقى في هذا البيت . . لا يريد أن يبقى حتى يرى كل ما حوله ينهار حتى أمه ... مثله الأعلى ... أرق وأسمى ماكان في حياته . . يريد أن يهرب . . يريد أن ينسى . . يريد أن يسكر . . وجرت خلفه وهي تولول : أحمد . . أحمد . . أحمد . . وخرجت لتلحق به على السُّلَّم ، وهي لا تزال تصيح : أحمد . . أحمد . . أحمد . .

(إحسان عبد القدوس – لا تطفيء الشمس ١٩٦٠. ص٤٣٢-٤٣٣)

He dashed from his room like a burning rocket ... He does not want to stay in this house ... He does not want to stay to see every thing around him falling apart even his mother ... his ideal ... the most delicate and most exalted he had in his life ... He wants to run away ... He wants to forget ... He wants to get drunk ... She followed him crying: Ahmad ... Ahmad ... Ahmad ... She went out to catch up with him on the steps while she was still shouting: Ahmad ... Ahmad ... Ahmad ...

Example 2:

عاد صلاح الى البيت وقذف كتبه ودفاتره الى الأرض بحركة حانقة . فسألته أمه : "ما بكَ ؟" فأجاب على الفور : "سئمت المدرسة" . فقالت الأم متسائلة بحنو : "ولماذا سئمت المدرسة ؟" . فصمت صلاح لحظة ثم قال : "أريد أن أتزوج" . وقالت الأم مخاطبة الأب بوجل : :هل لك اعتراض ؟" . فلم يأبه الأب لسؤالها انما التفت نحو صلاح وقال له بصوت قاس : "أنت ولد عاق ولا تستحق أن أوافق على زواجك" . فقال صلاح بضراعة : "سأكون منذ هذه اللحظة ابناً باراً مطيعاً" .

– ستصلي ؟
– سأواضب على الصلاة
– ستصلي خمس مرات في اليوم ؟
– سأصلي خمس مرات
– ستصوم شهر رمضان ؟
– سأصوم شهر رمضان كله

- لن تسهر خارج البيت ؟
- لن أسهر وسأنام كل ليلة باكراً
- لن تسكر ؟
- لن أسكر وسأذهب الى مكة سيراً على الأقدام
ففرح وجه الأب وقال : "تعال قبِّل يدي" . فدنا صلاح من أبيه وأحنى رأسه وقبَّل يده بخشوع . وبعدئذ ضحك الأب بابتهاج وقال : "الآن قل لي من تريد ان تتزوج ؟"

(زكريا تامر – الرعد ١٩٧٨ ص٧١-٧٢)

Salah came back home and threw with anger his books and exercise books on the floor. His mother asked him: "What is wrong?" He immediately answered: "I am fed up with school." His mother compassionately asked him: "And why are you fed up with school?" Salah kept silent for a while and replied: "I want to get married." The mother spoke with fear to the father: "Do you have any objection?" The father did not show any interest in her question and turned towards Salah and said: "You are a disobedient son and do not deserve my agreement on your marriage." Salah said humbly:"I shall be from this moment an obedient and pious son."
- Will you pray?
- I shall always observe my prayers.
- Will you pray five times a day?
- I shall pray five times.
- Will you keep the fast of Ramadan?
- I shall fast all Ramadan.
- Will you not stay out late at night?
- I shall not stay late at night and I shall go to bed early every night.
- Will you drink alcohol?
- I shall not drink alcohol and I shall go to Mecca on foot.

The father's face looked happy and he said: "Come and kiss my hand." Salah came towards him, bent his head, and kissed his hand humbly. After that the father laughed happily and said: "Now tell me who do you want to marry?"

Folktales are referred to in Arabic as (طرائف) which are prototypically characterized by the use of an initial passive verbal sentence, i.e., it starts with a verb in the passive form, such as (قيل أنَّ - it was said that, حُكِيَ أنَّ ، يُروى أنَّ - it was narrated that), the start of the second and some other sentences with the additive conjunctive element (فـ - and), dialogue turns beginning with (فقال - and he said), synonymy and near synonymy, and reiteration of some lexical items.

Example 3:

يروى أنَّ أحد المُغفَّلين خرج يوما من منزله فعثر في طريقه على قتيل فجرَّه حتى أوصله إلى منزله ، وهناك القاه في بئر كان مهجورا ، فعلِمَ أبوه بذلك فخاف على إبنه ، فغيَّبه ثم أخذ كبشا وخنقه وألقاه في البئر وأهال علَيه التراب . ثم إنَّ أهل القتيل طافوا في الشوارع والأزقة يبحثون عنه فلقيهم المُغفَّل المذكور وقال : في دارنا رجل مقتول فانظروا أهو صاحبكم ؟ فعدلوا إلى المنزل وأنزلوه في البئر ، فلما رأى الكبش ناداهم قائلا : يا هؤلاء هل كان لصاحبكم قرون ؟ فضحكوا منه وتركوه بعد أن رأوا الكبش وقرونه .

(مجلة العربي : ص١٣١ العدد ٢١٦ نوفمبر (تشرين ٢) ١٩٧٦)

There is a tale about a simpleton who went out one day and came across someone who had been murdered. Then he dragged him to his (the simpleton's) house and dropped him in an abandoned well. When his father found out, he got concerned for his son and decided to keep him away from people for some time. Then he took a ram, suffocated it, and then dropped it in the same well and dropped some mud on it. Later on, the family of the victim started asking everyone in every street. Suddenly, the simpleton met them and told them: "There is someone murdered in our house. Come and look whether it is the one you are looking for". They decided to go to his house and then they put him in the well. When the simpleton saw the dead ram, he asked them: "You! Does your friend have horns?". They started laughing and left him after they saw the dead ram with its horns.

Example 4:

حُكيَ أنَّ أحد الملوك كان على طعام ، فأقبل أحد الخدم وبيده صحن فيه طعام ، فعثر الخادم فوقع شيء يسير من الطعام على ثياب الملك ، فاحتدَّ الملك وأمر بضرب عنقه ، فما كان من الخادم إلاَّ أنْ صبَّ جميع ما كان في الصحن على ثياب الملك فقيل له : "ويحك ما هذا ؟". فقال : "إنما فعلت ذلك لئلا يقول الناس قتله بغير ذنب ، وبهذا أصون عرض الملك وأقيم له عذرا". فأطرق الملك ساكتا هنيئة ثم عفى عنه وأعتقه .

(مجلة العربي : ص١٣٤ العدد ٢١٥ أكتوبر (تشرين ١) ١٩٧٦)

It was said that a king was having his meal. One of the king's servants holding a plate full of food passed by him. The servant stumbled and a little amount of food dropped on the king's dress. The king got furious and demanded that this servant should be hit on the neck. When the servant heard this, he poured all the plate on the king's dress. When the servant was asked why he did that, he replied: "I have done this for fear of your reputation so that people will not accuse you of killing me for no reason. Therefore, I have provided a reason for you". The king thought for a while and then pardoned him and released him as a free man.

Example 5:

دُعي أحد أطباء الأطفال إلى مأدُبة عشاء ، فالتفَّت حوله الأمهات من المدعوات ورحن يضايقنه بالأسئلة الخاصة بصحة أطفالهن . وعندما سألته إحداهن عن المرض الرئيسي للأطفال ، أجاب في عصبية : "الأمهات".

(مجلة العربي : ص٦٤ العدد ٣٦٨ يوليو (تموز) ١٩٨٩)

A paediatrician was once invited to a dinner party and was surrounded by the invited mothers to the same party. They kept asking him questions about children's health and he got very annoyed. When one of the mothers asked him about the main disease that affect children, he angrily replied: "Mothers".

Example 6:

عاد رجل مريضاً ، فلما خرج قال لأهله : "أحسن الله عزائكم". فقالوا : "إنَّه لم يمت". قال : "أعرف ، ولكنني شيخٌ كبير لا أستطيع النهوض في كل وقت ، وأخاف أنْ يموت فأعجز عن المجيء لأُعزِّيكُم به" .

(مجلة العربي : ص٦٥ اعدد ٣٦٨ يوليو (تموز) ١٩٨٩)

A man went to visit a sick person at his house. When the man left, he said to the sick person's family: "My condolences". "But he has not died, yet", they replied. The man said: "I know but I am an old man and cannot come again. So just in case he dies and I cannot come, I offer my condolences to you in advance".

2. Drama (المسرحية): This type of text involves serious comic and historical plays. The dramatic dialogue is usually written for the stage where the characters produce the language as natural speech. In terms of stylistic features, the language of dramatic texts, like prose fiction, is prototypically modern standard Arabic. The stylistic hallmarks of dramatic texts are the choice of emotive, figurative, and connotative expressions, presentation, some colloquial or foreign words, synonymy and near synonymy.

Example 1:

بلقيس : أجلس أولاً .
منذر : لقد تعبت من الجلوس .
بلقيس : هنا . . هنا . . كلبي الأمين يجب أن يخر دائماً عند أقدامي .
منذر : (وهو يجلس عند قدميها) ماذا تريدين الآن ؟
بلقيس : أن تتبعني في كل مكان .
منذر : وهل أستطيع غير ذلك ؟
بلقيس : ستذهب معي الى الملك سليمان .
منذر : سلاسلي في يديك ، تستطيع أن تشدني أينما تذهبين .
بلقيس : ليس يرضيني أَن أقول هناك عنك إنكَ أسيري .

منذر : وماذا يرضيك أن تقولي ؟
بلقيس : أريد لك لقباً رفيعاً .
منذر : أرفع من لقب "كلبك" ؟
(توفيق الحكيم – سليمان الحَكيم ١٩٥٧ ص ٥٩)

Bilqis: Sit down first.
Munthir: I am tired of sitting down.
Bilqis: Here ... here ... My faithful dog should always sit by my feet.
Munthir: (sitting down by her feet) What do you want?
Bilqis: To come with me wherever I go.
Munthir: Do I have another choice?
Bilqis: You will come with me to King Suleiman.
Munthir: My chains are in your hand and can tie me wherever you go.
Bilqis: It does not please me to tell them there that you are my prisoner of war.
Munthir: What is it that pleases you to say?
Bilqis: I want to give you a senior title.
Munthir: More senior than the title "your dog"?

4.2.4.2 Non-Fictional نص غير قصصي

Texts on history (النصوص التأريخية) are regarded as non-fictional texts. The hallmarks of non-fictional history texts are factual historical names, places, years, and information, the use of reiteration of lexical items, the use of emotive and figurative expressions, and the description in the third person, as in:

Example 1:

مرَّ النضال العربي ما بين ١٩٤٨ و ١٩٦١ بثلاث مرَاحل : الأولى من سنة ١٩٤٨ – ١٩٥٤ . وقد شهدت الإنقلابات المتتالية في سوريا من إنقلاب حسني الزعيم الى إنتهاء دكتاتورية الشيشكلي ، وثورة مصر سنة ١٩٥٢ ، وانتفاضتين في العراق سنة ١٩٤٨ ، وسنة ١٩٥٢ ، ومعركة شعبية في الأردن سنة ١٩٥٤ ، ضد مؤامرات الإستعمار وأنها مرحلة القلق والنقمة التي عقبت النكبة . الثانية من سنة ١٩٥٤ الى سنة ١٩٥٨ ، وقد شهدت التقاء وفدي مصر وسورية في مؤتمر باندونج ، وانبثاق السياسة العربية المتحررة ، كما شهدت خروج مصر الثورة على سياسة إحتكار الأسلحة ، ومقاومة حلف بغداد ومعركة قنال السويس وقيام حكومة وطنية في الأردن ، وصمود سوريا أمام المؤامرات الإستعمارية . وشهدت أيضاً نكسة الأردن الرجعية . الثالثة من سنة ١٩٥٨ الى سنة ١٩٦١ ، وقد شهدت قيام وحدة مصر وسورية ، وثورة لبنان ، وثورة العراق وانحراف هذه الثورة ، ومحاولات الإستعمار والرجعية العربية لتفكيك عُرى الوحدة .
(ناجي علوش – الثورة والجماهير ص ١٠ في ١٩٦٠)

The Arab struggle between 1948 and 1961 passed through three stages: the first was from 1948-1954 which witnessed successive coups in Syria - from Husni al-Za'im's coup till the end of al-Shishkly's dictatorship, Egypt's revolution in 1952, two uprisings in Iraq in 1948 and in 1952, a popular uprising in Jordan in 1954, against the colonialists' plots. It was the stage of concern and vengeance which followed the disaster. The second was from 1954-1958 which witnessed the meeting of Syrian and Egyptian delegations in the Bandong Conference and the birth of liberal Arab politics, Egypt's revolt against the policy of weapons monopoly, resistance of the Baghdad Pact, the Suez Canal war, the establishment of a nationalist government in Jordan, the Syrian defiance against colonialists' plots, and the reactionary Jordanian relapse. The third was from 1958-1961 which witnessed the establishment of the union between Egypt and Syria, revolution in the Lebanon, revolution in Iraq, the deviation of Iraq's revolution, and the attempts by the colonialists and the reactionary Arabs to dismantle the bonds of the union.

Example 2:

كان التنازُع بين الدويلات الإسلامية في شمال أفريقيا قد أضعفها وجعلها هدفاً لحملات الأسبانيين والبرتُغاليين الذين احتلوا أجزاء من مناطقها الساحلية المختلفة . فاستنجد الجزائريون بالبحاريْن المسلميْن المشهوريْن عروج وأخيه خير الدين بربروسا . فقدما إلى الجزائر وتمكنا من صد حملة أسبانية ضدها . ثم خرج عروج إلى البحر لقتال الأسبان فقُتِلَ في إحدى المعارك . وانفرد أخوه بحكم الجزائر . وأمده السلطان سليم الأولَ بقوات مكنته من السيطرة على مقاليد الأمور داخل بلاده ، وطرد الأسبان من معاقلهم القريبة منها وذلك عام ٩٥٢هـ . وأصبحت تلك البلاد ولاية عثمانية . وعُيِّن خير الدين والياً عليها ، وقائداً للأسطول العثماني في تلك المنطقة . وقد تمكن ، فيما بعد ، من الإستيلاء على تونس وإدخالها تحت حكم الدولة العثمانية . ولقد استنجد الليبيون بالسلطان العثماني سليمان القانوني ليُخلِّصهم من احتلال نصارى مالطة لبلادهم ، فأرسل قوة طردت أولئك المحتلين من ليبيا ، وذلك عام ٩٥٨ هـ . وهكذا أصبحت بلدان شمال أفريقيا : الجزائر وتونس وليبيا ولايات عثمانية .

(جوانب من تأريخ المسلمين . المملكة العربية السعودية / وزارة المعارف . ص ٣٦ عام ٢٠٠٠)

The dispute between the Muslim statelets in North Africa weakened them and made them a target to campaigns by the Spanish and the Portuguese who occupied different parts of their coastal areas. The Algerians solicited the help of the two well-known Muslim sailors Aruj and his brother Khair Al-Din Barbarossa who came to Algeria and were successful to stop a Spanish campaign against it. Then, Aruj went to the sea to fight against the Spanish and was killed in one of the battles. His brother became the sole ruler of Algeria. Sultan Salim I supplied him with forces which enabled him to control the internal state of affairs and expel the Spanish from their fortifications near

Algeria in 259 AH. This country, therefore, had become an Ottoman province and Sultan Khair Al-Din was appointed its governor and the commander of the Ottoman fleet in that region. After that, he managed to conquer Tunisia and put it under the Ottoman rule. The Libyans solicited the help of the Ottoman Sultan Suleiman the Law-Giver to rescue them from the rule of the Christians of Malta in 859 AH. Thus, the North African countries, Algeria, Tunisia and Libya, had become Ottoman provinces.

4.2.5 Letter Text نص الرسالة

4.2.5.1 Formal Letters الرسائل الرسمية

Formal letters are free from figurative, connotative and emotive expressions. On the grammatical level, they are marked by short sentences. Reiteration of lexical expressions is employed as in recommendation letters. Modes of address differ according to the position of the person the letter is addressed to (see 2.13 Modes of Address).

Example 1:

التاريخ : 1 / 01 / 2000 إفرنجي

الموضوع / شهادة تعريف
تشهدُ شركة راس لانوف لتصنيع النفط والغاز بأن الأخ / حسين محمد أبو سيف
هو أحد مستخدميها منذالتاريخ : 1 / 04 / 1993 إفرنجي وهو يعمل حاليا على وظيفة
مترجم
أُعطيت له هذه الإفادة بناءاً على طلبه لإستعمالها في الأغراض القانونية .
والسلام عليكم ورحمة الله وبركاته

محمد محمد عبدالله
مدير إدارة الشؤون الإدارية

Date: 1/01/2000 AD
Subject: Work Certificate
Ras Lanuf Oil and Gas Processing Company hereby certifies that Mr Hussein Abu Seif is one of its employees since 1/4/1993 AD and currently holds the position of translator.
This certificate has been given to him upon his request to be used for legal purposes only.
Peace and blessings of God be upon you.
Muhammad Muhammad Abdullah
Manager of Administration Department

Example 2:

التأريخ : ١٦/٨/١٩٩٩
الرقم : ٢٧٠٠

السيد مدير الشؤون الإدارية
بعد التحية

إشارة الى كتابكم المرقم ٣٣٧٤ والمؤرخ في ٢٨/٧/١٩٩٩ بشأن إيفاد السيد نجم أحمد إبراهيم الى بريطانيا في دورة تدريبية في مجال صيانة الأجهزة لمدة ٣٦ إسبوعاً إعتباراً من ٢٥/١٠/١٩٩٩ في جامعة ليدز .

عليه نُفيدكم بالموافقة على إيفاده في هذه الدورة واتخاذ الإجراءات اللازمة بهذا الخصوص.

والسلام عليكم ورحمة الله وبركاته

(إمضاء)
حمد الأسود
مدير قسم الصيانة

Date: 16/8/1999
Number: 2700

To: Head of Administration
After greetings,

Further to your letter number 3374 of 28/7/1999 regarding the sending of Mr Najim Ahmad Ibrahim to Britain for a training course in maintenance of equipment for 36 weeks from 25/10/1999 in the University of Leeds.
Therefore, we inform you of the approval to send him to this course and to take the necessary procedures in this regard.
Peace and blessing of God be upon you

(signature)
Hamad Al-Aswad
Head of Maintenance Department

4.2.5.2 Informal Letters الرسائل غير الرسميَّة

These include such texts as: (i) letters between relatives and friends, (ii) postcard writing. The translations of these two types of writing are literal in order to render faithfully the Arabic text emotive expressions. Informal letters and postcards are characterized by the use of idiomatic expressions like (اليُمن والبركة - prosperity and blessing ، فراقك الغالي - your precious absence).

Idiomatic expressions which are used to conclude an informal letter are like (مع تحيات - with best regards, ودُمتم في أمان الله - May you remain in God's protection). Modes of address differ according to whether the letter is sent to a family member or to a friend (see 2.13 Modes of Address).

(i) Letters الرسائل الشخصيّة

Example 1:

١٥ يوليو ١٩٩٩

أخي العزيز خالد

بدأنا نقلق عليك كثيراً وخاصة الوالدة فمنذ مدة طويلة لم نسمع صوتك ولم نستلم أي رسالة منك وزاد قلقنا عندما سمعنا من صديقك هشام بانك إنتقلت الى مدينة أخرى بحثاً عن قبول هناك . أرجو منك الكتابة وإخباري بأحوالك لكي أطمأن وأرتاح نفسياً . كلنا قلقون عليك ونريد أن نعرف بأن كل شيء على ما يُرام . أما بالنسبة لي فأنا بخير والحمد لله والوالدة كذلك ولا يهمنا سوى فراقك الغالي علينا فأنت شمعة البيت .

أسأل الله تعالى أن يحفظك ويحقق طموحاتك العلمية .
مع تحيات

أخوكَ المخلص
عماد

15 July 1999
Dear brother Khalid,
We have begun to feel very worried about you especially my mother since for a long time we have neither heard your voice nor received any letter from you. Our concern increased when we heard from your friend Hisham that you moved to another city looking for acceptance there. Please write to me and tell me how things are with you so that I feel assured and psychologically comfortable. We are all worried about you and want to know that everything is fine. As for me, I am fine, thank God, and so is mum. We are not concerned about anything except your valuable absence for us because you are the candle of the house.
I pray to God to protect you and enable you achieve your academic aspirations.

Best regards
Your sincere brother
Imad

Example 2:

أُختي العزيزة مريم المحترمة
تحية عطرة أهديك وأُقبِّل عيون الأطفال وأُسلِّم على الأخ أبو هدى المحترم وأتمنى أن تكونوا بألف خير . لقد بعثت قبل إسبوعين أو أكثر رسالة وأتمنى أنها قد وصلتكِ . قبل عدة أيام أتى محمد عندنا وبقي عندنا يومان ورجع وأنه والحمد لله بصحة جَيدة وأمي أيضاً صحتها جيدة ولكنها قلقة لأن محمد وبناته قد أزعجوها .
قد فتحت المدارس ولم يبقى إلا شهران والسنة الدراسية تنتهي ومصطفى ناجح في نصف السنة ولكن نورا تعاني من درسان وأنني أيضاً في البيت وقد قدمت أوراقي لغرض التعيين ولكن المستمسكات غير كافية ربما أستطيع أن أكملها في الصيف . وقد ألهي نفسي بشؤون البيت وفي بعض الأحيان أذهب لزيارة الجوارين ولكن الوقت لا ينتهي .
البنات يطلبون منك أن ترسلي لنا صورة بلال . أتمنى أن تبعثيها لنا .
اليوم عطلة رسمية لَمناسبة صدور بيان آذار وكلنا في البيت وركَّبْت كُبة جريش مثل ما تفعله أمي (مكانكِ خالي) . وكانت طيبة جداً .
نستعد الآن للعيد ولاندريٍ هل أمي تأتي أم لا . أرجو أن تستمري في المراسلة ولا تنقطعي عنا لكي نسمع أخباركِ لأن الرسالة نصف اللقاء وجزء مكمل من العلاقة الأخوية بيننا .

أختكِ
سلمى أحمد البغداديَ
٢٠٠٠/٣/٢
(إمضاء)

My dear respected sister,
I offer you a perfumed greeting and kiss the eyes of the children and send my greetings to the brother Huda's father, esquire, and hope you are in prosperity a thousand times more. I sent two or more weeks ago a letter and hope you have received it. A few days ago Muhammad came to our house and stayed for two days and went back; he is, thank God, in good health, and so is my mother but she is upset because Muhammad and his daughters annoy her. Schools have re-opened and there are only two months left for the academic year to finish. Mustafa has passed his first term but Nora is struggling with two modules. I am staying at home and sent my documents to get a job but the documents were not complete. I may be able to complete them during the summer. I keep myself busy with the housework and sometimes I go out to visit neighbours but time is endless.

The girls ask you to send us Bilal's photo. I wish you would send it to us.
Today is a national holiday which is the occasion of the March Declaration and all of us are at home. I have cooked crushed grain Kubbah just as my mother cooks it (your place is empty). It was delicious.
We are now getting ready for the Eid and we do not know whether my mother will come or not. Please continue writing to us and do not stop in order to hear your news because the letter is half of the meeting and a complementary part of our sisterly relations between us.

Your sister
Salma Ahmad Al-Baghdadi
2/3/2000
(signature)

(ii) Postcards البطاقات

Example 1:

أُختي العزيزة سعاد المحترمة
لمناسبة عيد الأضحى المبارك أهديكِ وأفراد عائلتي جميعاً تحياتنا العطرة وللأخ أبو نياز والأولاد جميعاً ، أعاده الله عَليكم وعلينا باليُمن والبركة .

ودمتم في أمان الله

أختك
إيمان عبدالمجيد
٢٠٠٠/٣/١١
(إمضاء)

Dear respected sister Su'ad,
On the occasion of the blessed Eid of the Sacrifice, I and all my family give you, brother Niyaz's father, and all the children our perfumed greetings as presents.
May God return it to you and to us with prosperity and blessing.
May you remain in God's protection.
Your sister
Eman Abdul-Majeed
11/3/2000
(signature)

Example 2:

نهديك جميعاً أعطر التحايا بمناسبة عيد الأضحى المبارك ، أعاده الله عليكَ وعلينا باليُمن والبركة .
لقد أرسلنا لكَ عدة رسائل ولكن لم نلق منكَ الرَّد على أية واحدة منها ، فنحن مشتاقون جداً لسماع أخبارك . نطلب منكَ أن ترسل لنا صورة وأنت في ليدز ونرجوا أن تبعثها لنا.
ودمت في أمان الله

بنات الأخت
(إمضاء)

Perfumed greeting
To our dear uncle Hussein,
All of us give you the most perfumed greetings on the occasion of the blessed Eid of the Sacrifice. May God return it to you and to us with prosperity and blessing.
We sent you many letters but you did not reply to any one of them. We are very eager to hear your news. We want you to send us your photo in Leeds and we ask you to kindly send it to us.
May you remain in Gods protection.
Nieces
(signature)

4.2.6 Poetry الشعر

There are two types of poetry: rhymed poetry (fixed rhyme) (الشعر المُقفَّى) and free verse (الشعر الحُر). Fixed rhyme refers to mono-rhyming poetry which is based on classical Arabic prosody (علم العروض), i.e., we still find the use of metre and rhyme but they are somehow simpler. Free poetry, however, is free from the strict rules of isometric lines. Free verse is the direct impact of European poetry and is characterized by uneven rhymes and simple language. However, both types of poetry are highly marked by figurative language, reiteration of lexical expressions and emotiveness. In terms of vocabulary and figurative language, the language of modern poetry is simpler and more straightforward than that of classical poetry. New modern words, concepts, imagery, and topics typical of contemporary environment are found in modern Arabic poetry.

Example 1:
Samples of rhymed poetry (الشعر المُقفَّى):

أكُلَّما عصفت بالشعب عاصفة هوجاء نستصرخ القرطاس والقلما

هل أنقذ الشام كتَّاب بما كتبوا   أو شاعر صان بغدادا بما نظما

(Palestine and Modern Poetry, 1984:76)

Why is it whenever a violent storm shakes us thoroughly we resort to pen and paper?

Did the writers or poets rescue Sham (Syria) or Baghdad by their writings?

هل جلست العصر مثلي   بين جفنات العنب
والعناقيد تدلَّت   كثريات الذهب
فهي للصادي عيونٍ   ولمن جاع الطعام
أعطني الناي وغنٍّ   وانس داءً ودواء
إنما الناس سطورٌ   كُتبت لكن بماء
ليت شعري أيَّ نفع   في اجتماع وزحام
وجدالٍ وضجيج   واحتجاجٍ وخصام ؟

(Bushrui, An Introduction to Khalil Gibran 1970:43)

Have you, like me, rested in the evening in the grape arbor,
The clusters hanging down like golden chandeliers?
For the thirsty, they are as springs, for the hungry, as food.
Give me the flute and sing! Forget distress and cure,
For people are lines which are written not with ink but water.
Would that I know what good there is in throng and crowd,
In strife and clamour, argument and quarrel.

Example 2:

Samples of free verse (الشعر الحُر):

لوِ كُنتِ يا حبيبتي
بمُستوىَ جُنوني
رميتِ ما عليْكِ من جواهر . .
وبعتِ ما لديكِ من أساورٍ
ونمتِ في عُيونيَ . .

(Kabbani, Arabian Love Poems 1993:23)

Oh, my love,
If you were at the level of my madness,
You would cast away your jewelry,
Sell all your bracelets,
And sleep in my eyes.

أصرخ أين شهامتكم ؟!!
إنْ كنتم عرباً . . . بشراً . . . حيوانات
فالذئبة حتى الذئبة ، تحرس نطفتها

والكلبة تحرس نطفتها
والنملة تعتز بثقب الأرض
وأما أنتم ،
فالقدس عروس عروبتكم !!

(Muzaffar al-Nawwab, in Nimrod: Arabic Literature: Then and Now, Vol. 24, No. 2, Spring 1981, p. 134)

I scream
Where is your gallantry?
If you are Arabs,
human beings,
animals,
The she-wolf
even the she-wolf
protects her young;
the she-dog
protects her young;
the ant even
takes pride
in a little hole in the ground.
As for you,
Jesusalem is your cherished bride
Hurrah!

4.2.7 Instructional Text النص الإرشادي

Instructional texts tell people what to do. Stylistically, they are free from emotive, connotative and figurative expressions. The other stylistic hallmarks of Arabic instructional texts are the use of the second person pronoun, the use of formulaic expressions, reiteration of lexical items, and the occurrence of nominal sentences (nominalization) which set the scene for the instructional statement and advice, as in example 1 instructional texts below, and as in (ولصحة وسلامة تفكيرك وأعصابك - for the health and safety of your thinking and nerves), and (وللحفاظ على صحة قلبك - for maintaining the health of your heart) in example 3, sample 1 below. There are two categories of instructional texts: the first is that which tells the reader/hearer how to do things, as in how to cook something, how to fix a fault, how to provide first aid. This category of instructional texts usually contains verbal imperative sentences and they appear in the form of a list of steps to be followed, as in example 3 samples 2 and 3 below. These sentences are action-demanding commands. Instructional texts can be either short texts of one word or one noun phrase as in example 1 samples, one or two short sentences for prescriptions issued by doctors as in example 2 samples, or can be long running texts as in example 3 samples.

Example 1:

Samples of short instructional texts:

قِفْ ! – Stop!

إِنْتَبِه ! – Watch out!

الهدوء رجاءاً – Quiet Please

الدخول ممنوع – No Entry

التدخين ممنوع – No Smoking

Example 2:

Samples of medical prescriptions (الوصفة الطبيَّة):

R/ lanoxin tab.

نصف قرص ٣ مرات يومياً
تقليل الملح بالطعام
إستشارة الطبيب بعد إسبوعين

Half a tablet 3 times a day
Reduce salt in food
Consult the doctor after 2 weeks

R/ Ampicilline 125 mg (susp.)

ملعقة صغيرة كل ٦ ساعات

Teaspoonful every 6 hours.

R/ Paracetamol infan. syrup.

ملعقة صغيرة ٣ مرات يومياً لحين إنخفاض الحرارة
عمل كمادات باردة إذا ارتفعت الحرارة الى ٤٠

One teaspoonful 3 times a day until temperature drops
Apply cold towels if temperature goes up to 40.

Note that the major hallmark of the above instructional prescription texts are the verbless 'sentences' and the use of nominalization like (تقليل - reduction; إستشارة - consultation; عمل - making). At the top of the prescription, Arab doctors usually use English expressions of the medicine.

Example 3:

Samples of extended instructional texts (نُصوص إرشاديَّة مُطوَّلة):

Sample 1:

هذه مجموعة من النصائح التي تهم كل إمرأة . بوسع الطب الحديث ياسيدتي أن يقدم لك الشيء الكثير للحفاظ على صحتك وجمالك ، ولن يُكلفك ذلك إلا شيئاً من الرغبة الأكيدة والإرادة الحازمة ، ولنبدأ منهجنا على الوجه التالي : أقلّي من التدخين فهو مُضر بجمالك فضلاً عن صحتك . وحذار من الإساءة الى شعر رأسك بالأصباغ والقص المتعاقب بشكل جنوني . كما أن ثغر المرأة من أبرز مواطن محاسنها فعليك بعدم التفريط بصحة اسنانك وحاولي جاهدة الإمتناع عن إقتلاع أي سن إلا للضرورة القصوى . ولصحة وسلامة تفكيرك وأعصابك عليك بالنوم المنتظم الكافي المريح . وإذا ما تجاوزت الأربعين كان لزاماً عليك الإقلال من السعرات الحرارية . وللحفاظ على صحة قلبك تجنبي الحركات المفاجئة العنيفة. وإذا كنت قد جاوزت الخامسة والثلاثين فمن المستحسن أن تطلبي الى طبيبتك أن تقوم مرة كل عام أو عامين بأخذ مسحة من عنق الرحم وفحصها للتأكد من عدم إصابتك – لا سمح الله – بسرطان الرحم .

(مجلة العربي : ص ٨٤–٨٧ العدد ٢٣٦ يوليو (تموز) ١٩٧٨)

This is a set of pieces of advice which are important to every woman. Modern medicine, my lady, can offer you a great deal to help you preserve your health and beauty. This will not cost you anything except definite willingness and determination. Let us start our programme as follows: cut down on smoking. It is harmful for your beauty let alone your health. Beware of abusing your hair with dying and cutting it regularly in a crazy manner. The woman's mouth is one of the most distinguished features of her beauty. Therefore, do not waste the beauty of your teeth and try not to pull out any tooth unless absolutely necessary. For the health and safety of your thinking and nerves, you have to have enough and comfortable regular sleep. If you are over forty, you have to reduce the number of calories. To maintain the health of your heart, avoid sudden and violent movements. If you are over thirty five, it is commended that you ask your (female) doctor to take a swab from the neck of your womb to examine it and make sure that you do not have – God forbid – cervical cancer.

Sample 2:

السلامة في السباحة

كثير من الناس يحبون الماء ، لكن معظمهم لا يجيدون السباحة . فهل تجيدها أنتَ ؟ قد تحاول السباحة أو يحاول أبناؤك ممارستها هذا الصيف . لكن قبل الإقدام على ذلك يجب أن نتذكر قواعد السلامة :

١. إحرص دائماً على أن يكون معك رفيق عندما تسبح ، فقد تحتاج الى معونة .
٢. لا تقترب من المياه العميقة إذا لم تكن سبّاحاً ماهراً .
٣. لا تسبح إذا كنت تشعر بالحر الشديد أو التعب .
٤. لا تسبح بعد الأكل مباشرة .

(مجلة العرب : ص ٨١ آب (أغسطس) ١٩٧٣)

Safety in Swimming
A lot of people like water but most of them are not good at swimming. Are you good at it? You may try this summer to swim or your children may try to. But before you decide to do so, you have to remember the safety rules:
1. Always try to have a companion with you when you swim. You may need some help.
2. Do not go to deep water if you are not a very good swimmer.
3. Do not swim if you feel extremely hot or tired.
4. Do not swim immediately after food.

Sample 3:

الحرائق لا تُطفأ بالدموع
١. لا تدع الأطفال يعبثون بعيدان الكبريت .
٢. إبعِد المواد القابلة للإشتعال عن مصادر النار المكشوفة .
٣. أبقَ بيتك ومكان عملك نظيفين من النفايات .
٤. لا تُدخن في الفراش ولا في الأماكن المحظورة .
٥. إحذر من أن تُحمِّل الدورات الكهربائية فوق طاقتها .
(مجلة العرب : ص ١٠٥٧ تموز (يوليو) ١٩٧٣)

Fire Cannot be Extinguished by Tears
1. Do not allow children play with matches.
2. Keep inflammable materials away from open fire.
3. Keep your house and office clean of litter.
4. Do not smoke in bed nor in the prohibited areas.
5. Be careful: Do not overload electrical circuits.

The second category of instructional texts are the legal texts (النص القانوني) such as a rent agreement, a contract, a resolution, a protocol, an agreement ratified by an international organization, etc., which tells people or the parties concerned what is expected of them and what to abide by. The major hallmarks of legal texts are the preamble (الديباجة), followed by an introduction (الفاتحة), then followed by the articles (المواد) of the agreement or convention, and finishes with a brief conclusion. We also find the use of a derived (subject-first) sentence structure as an initial sentence in the preamble, the recurrent use of structure number 61 (verb + subject + أنْ + verb-first sentence) also in the preamble, the use of nominalization in articles (جعل ، تحقيق ، إنماء ، حفظ), use of lexical cohesion through reiteration of some lexical items as in (وزير ، وزراء ، العمل ، القانون) and

(ميثاق ، هيئة ، إنسانية ، شعوب ، أنفسنا), clarity of language, lack of figurative or emotive expressions, use of passive sentences in the conclusion (وُضِعَ ، كُتِبَ), use of first person plural in the preamble (نحن - we), (أصدرنا - we have issued; ننقذ - we save; نؤكد - we affirm), and use of third person in the articles of the legal text.

Example 1:

قانون إتحادي رقم ٨ لسنة ١٩٨٠.
في شأن تنظيم علاقات العمل
الديباجة
نحن زايد بن سلطان آل نهيان رئيس دولة الإمارات العربية المتحدة ، بعد الإطلاع على أحكام الدستور المؤقت ، وعلى القانون رقم ١ لسنة ١٩٧٢ في شأن إختصاصات الوزارات وصلاحيات الوزراء ، وبناءاً على ما عرضه وزير العمل والشؤون الإجتماعية ،
أصدرنا القانون التالي :
المادة الأولى : لايجوز إستخدام غير المواطنين بقصد العمل في دولة الإمارات إلا بعد موافقة دائرة العمل .
المادة الثانية : يجب على صاحب العمل قبل تشغيل أي حدث أن يستحصل منه على موافقة كتابية ممن له الولاية أو الوصاية على الحدث .
المادة الثالثة : يُحضر تشغيل النساء في الأعمال الخطرة أو الشاقة أو الضارة صحياً .
كُتبَ هذا القانون في ٢٥ يوليو (تموز) ١٩٨٠. ويعمل به فوراً
(قانون رقم ٨ لعام ١٩٨٠ الخاص بتنظيم علاقات العمل في دولة الأمارات العربية المتحدة : ص ٢١)

Federal Law No. 8 of 1980
on the Regulation of Labour Relations
Preamble
We, Zayed bin Sultan Al Nihayyan the President of the United Arab Emirates, having taken cognizance of the provisions of the interim constitution, and of the Law No. 1 of 1972 regarding the jurisdiction of ministries and the powers of ministers, and according to the submission made by the Minister of Employment and Social Affairs, we have issued the following Law:
Article One: Non-nationals may be employed in the United Arab Emirates only after the approval of the Labour Department.
Article Two: The employer, before employing any minor, must obtain from him a written consent from his guardian.
Article Three: Women are prohibited to be employed in hazardous or arduous duties or duties which are health hazard.
This Law is issued on 25 July 1980 and should be applied immediately.

Example 2:

ميثاق الأمم المتحدة

الديباجة

نحن شعوب الأمم المتحدة ، وقد آلينا على أنفسنا

أنْ ننقذ الأجيال المقبلة من ويلات الحرب التي في خلال جيل واحد جلبت على الإنسانية مرتين أحزاناً يعجز عنها الوصف ،

وأن نؤكد من جديد إيماننا بالحقوق الأساسية للإنسان وبكرامة الفرد ،

وأن نبين الأحوال التي يمكن في ظلها تحقيق العدالة ،

وأن ندفع بالرقي الإجتماعي قُدُماً ،

وأن نرفع مستوى الحياة في جو من الحرية أفسح ،

وفي سبيل هذه الغايات إعتزمنا

أن نأخذ أنفسنا بالتسامح ،

وأن نعيش معاً في سلام وحسن جوار ،

وأن نستخدم الأداة الدولية في ترقية الشؤون الإقتصادية والإجتماعية للشعوب جميعاً ،

قد قررنا

أن نوحد جهودنا لتحقيق هذه الأغراض .

المادة الأولى

١. حفظ السلم والأمن الدوليين
٢. إنماء العلاقات الودية بين الأمم
٣. تحقيق التعاون الدولي على حل المسائل الدولية ذات الصبغة الأقتصادية والإجتماعية والثقافية والإنسانية
٤. جعل هذه الهيئة مرجعاً لتنسيق أعمال الأمم

المادة الثانية

١. تقوم الهيئة على مبدأ المساواة في السيادة بين جميع أعضائها .
٢. يفض جميع أعضاء الهيئة منازعاتهم الدولية بالوسائل السلمية .
٣. يمتنع أعضاء الهيئة جميعاً في علاقاتهم الدولية عن التهديد باستعمال القوة أو إستخدامها .

المادة الثالثة

وُضِعَ هذا الميثاق بلغات خمس . ويظل الميثاق في محفوظات حكومة الولايات المتحدة الأمريكية .

وقد وقَّع مندوبو حكومات "الأمم المتحدة" على هذا الميثاق مصداقاً لما تقدم .

صدر بمدينة سان فرانسسكو في اليوم السادس والعشرين من شهر يونيو سنة ١٩٤٥ .

(ميثاق الأمم المتحدة : ١٩٤٥ ص ٩٢٣)

Charter of the United Nations

Preamble

We the peoples of the United Nations,
determined
to save succeeding generations from the scourge of war, which twice in our lifetime has brought untold sorrow to mankind, and
to affirm faith in fundamental human rights and in the dignity and worth of the human person, and
to establish conditions under which justice can be established, and
to promote social progress and better standards of life in larger freedom,
and for these ends
to practise tolerance, and
to live together in peace with one another as good neighbours, and
to employ international machinery for the promotion of the economic and social advancement of all peoples,
have resolved to combine our efforts to accomplish these aims.

Article 1

1. To maintain international peace and security.
2. To develop friendly relations among nations.
3. To achieve international cooperation in solving international problems of an economic, social, cultural, or humanitarian character.
4. To be a centre for harmonizing the actions of nations.

Article 2

1. The organization is based on the principle of the sovereign equality of all its Members.
2. All Members shall settle their international disputes by peaceful means.
3. All Members shall refrain in their international relations from threat or use of force.

Article 3

The present Charter is written in five languages and shall remain deposited in the archives of the Government of the United States of America.
IN FAITH WHEREOF the representatives of the Governments of the United Nations have signed the present Charter.
DONE at the city of San Francisco the twenty-sixth day of June, one thousand nine hundred and forty-five.

4.2.8 Descriptive Text النص الوصفي

Descriptive texts are subjective, i.e., they reflect the personal points of view of the writer/speaker. Therefore, the details provided are subjective. In Arabic descriptive texts, we find the first person singular/plural and sometimes the second person singular/plural used. Emotive, connotative, and figurative expressions are the hallmarks of descriptive texts. Hyperbolic and comparative styles are also expected in descriptive texts.

Example 1:

العين . . مصيف أبو ظبي
إتجهنا الى مدينة العين السياحية ذات الوجه الأخضر وهي مصيف أهالي أبو ظبي . وتقع في قلب المنطقة الشرقية ، وتبعد عن العاصمة أبو ظبي حوالي ١٦٠ كيلومترا . والعين كما رأيناها تعيش في حركة تطور زراعية وعمرانية وسياحية .وتتبعها في ذلك مجموعة من الضواحي هي المعترض ، المويجعي ، الجيمي وهيلي . وقد إرتبط إسمٍ هذه المدينة بأسم رئيس الدولة الذي إهتم بها خلال توليه حكم هذه المنطقة . ونظراً لكثرة أشجارها فقد كانت تجمع معظم السكان خلال الصيف هرباً من رطوبة الجو الزائدة في مدينة أبو ظبي . إنها مدينة تأريخية قديمة . يدل على ذلك وجود حضارة فوق أرضها تعود الى الألف الثالث قبل الميلاد . ومنذ القدم أيضاً ، إشتغل سكان العين بالزراعة فنجحت زراعة النخيل وبعض الأشجارَ الحمضية كالليمون والمانجو . ويحيط بمدينة العين ٢٠ ألف دونم من الأراضي الرملية زُرِعت كلها بالأشجار . ومما يستوقف الزائر لمدينة العين تلك المزارع الممتدة علىَ مدى البصر رغم البيئة الصحراوية التي تحيط بالمدينة .
(مجلة العربي : ص ٧٩ –٨٣ العدد ٢١٤ سبتمبر (أيلول) ١٩٧٦)

Al-Ain ... Abu Dhabi's Summer Resort
We headed to Al-Ain, the tourist city, with a green face. It is the summer resort of Abu Dhabi people. It is situated in the heart of the Eastern District and is 160 kilometres from the capital Abu Dhabi. Al-Ain, as we saw it, enjoys development in agriculture, construction, and tourism. The other suburbs which come after it are Al-Mu'tarid, Al-Muwej'i, Al-Jimi, and Hili. The name of this city is linked to the name of the head of state who gave it considerable attention when he was its ruler. Due to the abundance of its trees, it attracts during the summer most of the population who escape from the excessive moisture in Abu Dhabi. It is an old historical city. This is indicated by the existence of a civilization on its soil which dates back to the third millennium BC. Since olden times, the people of Al-Ain have worked in agriculture. The cultivation of date palms and some citrus fruit trees such as lemon and mango has been a success. Al-Ain is surrounded by 20000 hectares of sand which is all planted with trees. The visitor to Al-Ain will be surprised by the farms which stretch as far as he/she can see in spite of the desert environment surrounding the city.

Example 2:

دودة الأرض
دودة الأرض العادية يتألف جسمها من حلقات ظاهرة وهذه الحلقات يتراوح عددها في الدودة البالغة ما بين ١٢٠ الى ١٧٥ حلقة . والفم نجده في مقدمة الجسم وله

شكل الهلال وهو يقبع تحت ما يشبه الشفة العليا . أن هذا الدود له قناة هضم مكتملة الشكل . والحلقات الظاهرة في الجسم أعدادها كبيرة . أما الشعرات الشائكة المتصلة بالحلقات من ألأسفل فتساعد الدودة على الحركة . وليس للدودة فك وليس فيها أسنان . وهذه الديدان تتنفس عن طريق جلدها . ولابد من بقاء الجلد رطباً ليتم هذا .

(مجلة العربي : ص ٢٩ العدد ١٨٥ أبريل (نيسان) ١٩٧٤)

Earth Worm

The body of the ordinary earth worm contains visible rings. The average number of these rings in a mature worm is between 120 to 175. We find the mouth at the beginning of the body and has a crescent shape and is situated under what looks like an upper lip. These worms have a complete digestive canal. The visible rings in the body are in great numbers. The thorny hairs underneath the rings help the worm to move. The worm has neither jaws nor teeth. It breathes through its skin which has to remain moist to achieve this.

4.2.9 Expository Text النص الإستعراضي

There are many types of expository texts. An expository text can be either a report summarizing an event like a summit, a meeting (summarizing minutes), an opening ceremony, a critical report prepared by an auditor about a department, a company, a factory, etc., a personal report about someone such as memoirs, a briefing report that gives instruction or information to people such as police/press/ministry briefing, a summarized report (an abstract or a synopsis) of a symposium, or of an academic research, a short/long definition, an essay, a book review, or a report that explains the aims and objectives of a course, programme, policy, plan, publisher. The major stylistic hallmarks of expository texts are reiteration of lexical expressions, the use of connotative, figurative, and emotive expressions, the occasional use of passive or periphrastic passive sentences, and the occasional use of asyndetic sentences.

Example 1:

ويقول الأستاذ عبدالله النصار المدير التنفيذي لشركة سدافكو بالرياض : قد يكون هناك نوع من الحرب بين شركات صغيرة تحاول أنْ تخلُق لها حصة من السوق وأنا أعتقد أن حرب الأسعار غير مجدية ولن تخلُق حصة للشركات التي سعت إلى إغراق السوق بأسعار متدنية وغير مربحة ، ووجود شركات صغيرة هو سبب المشكلة وأرى الآن أن الدمج هو الأفضل ، يتم دمج شركات صغيرة معاً لتكون شركة كبيرة منافسة ، ولو رجعنا للمُستهلك السعودي نجده من أضعف دول العالم

إستهلاكاً للحليب واللبن ومشتقاته بسبب عدم وجود وعي كاف لديه بأهمية اللبن الغذائية وأنا أُحمِّل شركات الألبان المسؤولية في قلة وعي المستهلك بهذه الأهمية الغذائية مما سبَّب وجود هدر كبير في المنتج قياساً على حجم الإستهلاك ، هذا بخلاف وجود طغيان للمشروبات الغازية بأسعار منافسة ومتدنية للغاية حتى قياساً على أسعار هذه المشروبات الغازية في الدول المجاورة مما يعني أن الحرب ليست بين شركات ومنتجي الألبان فقط .
(جريدة الرياض : ص ٣٢ في ٢٠٠٠/٣/٦)

Mr Abdullah al-Nassar, the Executive Manager of Sadaf Co., Riyadh, said: There may be some kind of war among small companies which try to find a share in the market. I believe the price war is futile and will not create a share for the companies which have tried to flood the market with very low and unprofitable prices. The existence of small companies is the reason for this problem. I think that merging is the best solution where small companies can merge to form a big competitive company. If we look at the Saudi customer, we will find him/her the weakest customer in the consumption of milk, yoghurt and its derivatives due to the lack of awareness among customers of the nutritious significance of the dairy products. I put the blame on the dairy companies for this lack of awareness which has led to the huge waste of the product compared to the volume of consumption. This is in contrast to the domination of fizzy drinks whose prices are more competitive and very low even in comparison with the prices of fizzy drinks in the neighbouring countries. This indicates that the war is not only between companies and other dairy producers.

Example 2:

العدوان والعنف نادراً ما يحدُث خلال نوبات الصرع بالرغم من الإعتقاد الخاطيء السائد منذ زمن طويل بكثرة حدوثه. معظم الأبحاث التي أكدت وجود علاقة إيجابية وطيدة بين الصرع والعنف تم إنتقادها لوجود كثير من السلبيات والأخذ عليها . ولكن وبرغم ذلك تتزايد الأدلة والبراهين التي تؤكد وجود مثل هذه العلاقة وإن العنف والعدوان يمكن أن يحدث نتيجة نشاط النوبات الصرعية عند الفرد دون وجود أي دوافع أخرى لمثل هذا السلوك . خطورة وأهمية العواقب القانونية والإعتبارات الطبية تحتم وجود معايير ومقاييس معتمدة وموثوق بها لتحديد وتشخيص حالات العُنف النادرة التي تحصل أثناء النوبات الصرعية .
(المجلة العربية للطب النفسي : ص ١٢ المجلد الرابع - العدد الأول أيار (مايو) ١٩٩٣)

Aggression or violence are extremely rare during epileptic seizures, though there has been an anti-factual belief for a long time that it is common. Most of the studies which gave support to a positive relationship between epilepsy and violence had been criticized for many drawbacks. Nevertheless, evidence is accumulating to the effect that there is such a relationship and that violence or aggression can take place as a result of epileptic seizures and without any other motives for such a behaviour. The serious medico-legal implications of such a link demands reliable and valid criteria to help diagnose those rare epileptic patients who commit violence solely due to their epilepsy.

Example 3:

قدَّم الدكتور أسامة الباز مستشار الرئيس حسني مبارك للشؤون السياسية أمس تقريراً إلى الرئيس حول نتائج مباحثاته الأخيرة في إسرائيل مع إيهود باراك رئيس الوزراء الإسرائيلي ، وصرح الدكتور الباز بأن باراك أبلغه تقديره الكبير لجهود الرئيس مبارك ومبادراته مِن أجل الحفاظ على قوة الدفع في عملية السلام ، وأنَّ رئيس الوزراء الإسرائيلي يرَى أنَّ هذه المبادرات جاءت في وقت حسَّاس ، لأنه يُتوقع أنْ تكون الأسابيع المقبلة حافلة فيما يتصل بتقدم العمليةالسلمية ، والفُرص المُتاحة لتحقيق هذا التقدم . وأوضح الباز أنَّ باراك تحدث عن توجُّه إسرائيلي للتفاوض وتحقيق تقدُّم على جميع المسارات بالتوازي ، في وقت واحد ، وأن رئيس وزراء إسرائيل يتفق مع الرئيس مبارك في أنه توجد الآن فرصة تأريخية يجب عدم إضاعتها ، لأنها ربما لا تُسنح ثانية ، ولذلك فقد أكد باراك للباز أنَّ إسرائيل لن تنتظر ظروفاً جديدة أو تغيراً في الأوضاع حتى تتحرك .

(الأهرام : ص ١ في ٢ مارس (آذار) ٢٠٠٠)

Dr Osama Al-Baz, President Husni Mubarak's political affairs adviser handed in yesterday a report to President Mubarak on the results of his recent talks which he held in Israel with the Israeli Prime Minister Ehud Barak. Dr Al-Baz stated that Mr Barak informed him of his great appreciation of the effort and initiatives made by Mr Mubarak to maintain the momentum of the peace process. The Israeli Prime Minister believes that these initiatives have come at a critical time because he expects the coming weeks to be full of events related to the progress of the peace process and the opportunities available to achieve this progress. Dr Al-Baz also explained that Mr Barak talked about an Israeli move for negotiations and the achievement of equal and simultaneous progress at all levels and that the Israeli Prime Minister was in agreement with President Mubarak about the fact that there was a historical opportunity now that should not be wasted since it might not be available again. Mr Barak stressed to Dr Al-Baz that Israel would not be waiting for new circumstances or a change in circumstances to make a move.

Example 4:

عُقد المؤتمر العربي السادس للطب النفسي في القاهرة ما بين ١٦-١٨ نوفمبر

(تشرين الثاني) ١٩٩٤ . وقد حضر المؤتمر ما يزيد على ٨٠٠ طبيب نفسي من العالم العربي ومختلف الدول وكان غنياً بالأبحاث العربية والدولية ، وقدَ أُعيد إنتخاب اللجنة التنفيذية لإتحاد الأطباء النفسانيين العرب على النحو التالي :
الرئيس / أ . د . أحمد عكاشة الأمين العام / أ . د . محمد أبو صالح
كما عُيِّن المُنسِّقين التالية أسماؤهم :
د . أسامة عثمان توكل / مُنسِّق مع الولايات المتحدة الأمريكية
د . سامي الطويل / مُنسِّق مع فرنسا
د . خالد ياسين / مُنسِّق مع المملكة المتحدة
كما تم إنتخاب مجلس إدارة جديد للإتِّحاد يضم عضوين مِن كل بلد عربي .
لقد تقرر عقد المؤتمر العربي السابع للطب النفسي في بيِروت في نوفمبر ١٩٩٦ وستنظمه الجمعية اللبنانية للأطباء النفسانيين .
(المجلة العربية للطب النفسي : ص ١١٩ المجلد السادس – العدد الأول أيار (مايو) ١٩٩٥)

The sixth Arab psychiatry conference was held in Cairo between 16-18 November 1994. It was attended by more than 800 Arab and international psychiatrists. It was rich with Arab and international papers. The executive committee of the Union of Arab Psychiatrists was re-elected as follows:
President / Professor Ahmad Akash
General Secretary / Professor Muhammad Abu Salih
Also the following coordinators were appointed:
Dr Usama Uthman Tawakkul / Coordinator with the USA
Dr Sami al-Tawil / Coordinator with France
Dr Khalid Yasin / Coordinator with the UK
A new Administrative Council for the Union was also elected. Two members from each Arab country will be represented in this Council.
It was decided that the seventh Arab psychiatry conference will be held in Beirut in November 1996 and will be organized by the Lebanese Psychiatrists Society.

Example 5:

إنَّ هذا القرار سيحقق عدة أهداف مستقبلية سيكون لها أثرها الإيجابي الملموس في القطاع النفطي السعودي وهي :
– توسيع وتطوير وزيادة أداء وطاقة المصافي
– إيجاد تكامل في الصناعة البترولية السعودية بدرجة أكمل وأكبر وأفضل
– إيجاد مزايا جديدة في التسويق خاصَّة الدولي بشكل أفضل
– إيجاد مرونة جيِّدة في العقود والإتفاقيات حولَ شراء البترول ومشتقاته مع العملاء
– إتاحة فرص تدريبية للعاملين في قطاعات النفط المختلفة بمن فيهم العاملون في "سمارك" بشكلٍ أوسع وعملي أفضل .

(المجلة : ص ٦٥ في ٢٧ يونيو (حزيران) ٣٠ يوليو (تموز) ١٩٩٣ العدد ٦٩٨)

This decision will achieve a number of future objectives which will have positive and tangible impact on the Saudi oil sector; these are:
- widening, developing, and increasing the performance of refinery's output.
- creating integration in the Saudi petrol industry to a better and more perfect degree.
- creating new features in marketing especially at international level in a better way.
- creating good flexibility in contracts and agreements on the purchase of oil and its derivatives with agents.
- allowing training opportunities for the workers in the various oil sectors including workers in "Samarik" on a better, larger and more practical scale.

Example 6:

يقدم الكتاب عرضاً تفصيلياً للثوب الفلسطيني والإختلافات فيه بين منطقة وأخرى في فلسطين ، ويقدم عرضا تأريخيّاً وفنياً لتطور شكل الثوب وجمالياته عبر تأريخ الأراضي المقدسة وكيف كان هذا التطور تعبيراً عن تطور تأريخي واجتماعي أيظاً . وقد زُوِّد الكتاب بلوحات مصورة للثوب الفلسطيني مُوضِّحة جمالياته وكيفية تصميمه .

(مجلة العربي : ص ١٩٥ العدد ٣٦٨ يوليو (تموز) ١٩٨٩)

The book presents a detailed account of the Palestinian dress and its differences from one area to another in Palestine. It also presents a historical and artistic account of the shape development of the dress, its decorative patterns throughout the history of the sacred land, and how this development also reflects the social and historical development. This book is supplemented by pictures of the Palestinian dress which show its beauty and methods of its design.

Example 7:

كامل مصطفى هو عميد كلية الفنون الجميلة بالإسكندرية . وُلدَ عام ١٩١٧ ودَرَسَ بالقاهرة حتى تخرج من كلية الفنون الجميلة عام ١٩٤١ (كان إسمها في ذلك الوقت مدرسة الفنون الجميلة العليا) وقد عمل بتدريس الفن منذ تخرّجه وسافر إلى إيطاليا بعد إنتهاء الحرب العالمية الثّانية ليعود أُستاذاً لفن التصوير الزيتي بكلية الفنون بالقاهرة عام ١٩٥٠ . وعندما أُنشئت كلية الفنون الجميلة بالإسكندرية عام ١٩٥٨ تولى منصب رئيس قسَم التصوير بها ، ثُمَّ أصبح عميداً لها عام ١٩٦٨ . وقد شُوهدت أعماله في عدد كبير من المعارض المصرية بأوربا .

(مجلَّة العربي : ص ١٥٢ العدد ٢٠٠ يوليو (تموز) ١٩٧٥)

Kamel Mustafa is the Dean of the College of Fine Arts in Alexandria. He was born in 1917 and studied in Cairo until he graduated from the Fine Arts College in 1941 (formerly known as The High School of Fine Arts). He worked as a teacher of art since his graduation and travelled to Italy after the second world war. Then, he came back as a lecturer in art of oil painting at the College of Arts in Cairo in 1950. When the College of Fine Arts in Alexandria was established in 1958, he occupied the post of Head of Department of Photography, then he became its Dean in 1968. His works have been seen in many Egyptian fairs in Europe.

4.2.10 Argumentative Text النص الحواري

Argumentative texts are usually referred to as (إفتتاحية - editorial, comment, رأي / آراء - points of view, or رسائل القُرّاء - letters of readers (i.e., letters to the editor) in Arabic newspapers or magazines. The main stylistic hallmarks of argumentative texts are the use of emotive and figurative words, reiteration of lexical expressions, the use of adversative and causal conjunctions, the use of emphatic particles (إنّ / أنّ), the use of first person plural pronoun which is implicit in the verb in order to involve the reader/hearer in the writer's/speaker's viewpoints, the use of causal conjunctions like (للأسف - unfortunately, ولسوء الحظ - unfortunately, ومن المُقلق - what is worrying) for emphatic contrast as part of substantiation of own ideas, and the use of nominal or prepositional phrases at sentence-initial position to set the scene for the reader/hearer. The main purpose of an argumentative text is to persuade the reader/hearer of an idea using emotive expressions whenever needed. From an Arabic stylistics point of view, we usually encounter three main types of argumentative texts: through-argumentative, counter-argumentative, and hortatory counter-argumentative. In the first argumentative text type, the writer/speaker presents a proposition in order to substantiate the major thesis of the argument. The text continues in substantiation by providing factual back-up details to psychologically prepare the reader/hearer for his/her conclusion (see example 1). In Arabic counter-argumentative texts, the writer/speaker first presents his/her opponent's point of view, as the thesis, then he/she pounces upon the opponent's views by attacking and refuting them through counter-claims, ideas, statistical information, etc., then he/she provides a conclusion as a further support for the counter-claim (see example 2). Hortatory counter-argumentative texts are those used in Friday prayer speeches and religious articles in newspapers or magazines (see example 3). The stylistic technique of the counter-argumentative text applies to the hortatory counter-argumentative text. The major purpose of the hortatory counter-argumentative text is to provide a religious advice and consolidate faith, i.e., exhortation; therefore, examples from the Qur'an and the Hadith are usually used as supporting examples to refute the opponent's viewpoint.

Example 1:

الحوار والجدل حول أي قضية ظاهرة صحية في أي مجتمع بل قد تكون أحيانا ضرورة . . فمن خلال الحوار الجاد المثمر يمكن الخروج بآراء وطروحات تُفيد القضايا وتساهم في حلها . . وفي الماضي حينما كان مجتمعنا هذا في بداية التكوين والتشكل لم يكن هناك تعليم بالمفهوم الصحيح لهذه المفردة ولا وعي كاف بشؤون الحياة وقضاياها ومع هذا كان الناس يطرحون همومهم وإن كانت بسيطة في ذلك الوقت على بساط البحث في التجمعات خصوصاً أثناء الولائم والمناسبات حيث تتسع دوائر النقاش والجدل ويُدلي كل بدلوه . . فتخرج إلى النور بعض القرارات نتيجة لتلك الحوارات حيث كان يُعطى الحكماء وأصحاب الرأي والمشورة في المجتمع الفرصةلقول الرأي المسموع . .

في عصرنا الحاضر ومع ازدياد الحياة تعقيداً والمصالح تشابكاً إزدادت تبعاً لذلك الحاجة للحوار والنقاش والمناصحة فأصبحت سمة من سمات تقدم الشعوب وتطورها لدرجة إنتشرت فيها مكاتب الرأي وبيوتات المشورة إنتشار النار في الهشيم واصبح من الصعب على الفرد الذي يقوم بعمل له إرتباط بمصالح الآخرين أن يتخذ قراراً بشكل فردي . .

وبالرغم من تلك الأهمية للحوار إلا أن البعض (للأسف) قد أساء إستخدام حقه في الطرح فخلط مابين الحوار الهادف المنطقي والجدل البيزنطي الذي قد يقود إلى الخروج عن أدبيات الحوار إلى تبادل الإتهامات والشتم والسب . . فلا الحوار صار حواراً . . ولا الرأي رأياً . .

من يرغب في رؤية تلك الأمثلة فما عليه إلا مشاهدة برامج الحوار في وسائل الإعلام العربية ليرى ويسمع ما يحدث بين المتحاورين وكيف يُدار الحوار . . !! وهذا خطأ فادح وفشل يتحمله مُعد ومقدِّم البرنامج . . فكم من برامج حوار إشتهرت بطرح حوارات خطيرة تَهم العالم كان مقدموها في مُنتهى الحكمة والهدوء وهم يديرون حوارات مع شخصيات وعلماء ومفكرين وسياسيين عالميين . .

إذاً من خلال وسائل الإعلام نستطيع أن نؤصل فن الحوار المتزن الهادف والمفيد لدى المشاهد العربي .

(الرياض : ص ١٦ الإثنين ٦ مارس ٢٠٠٠)

Dialogue and debate about any matter are not only healthy phenomena in any society but can sometimes be a necessity ... Through serious and fruitful dialogue we can develop ideas and reach solutions beneficial to problems and can contribute in solving them ... In the past when our society was at the beginning of its formation, there was neither adequate education about this particular word nor was there enough awareness of the worldly affairs of life. In spite of that, people during gatherings used to debate their concerns, which were not complicated at that time, especially during banquets and occasions where debate and discussion could be widened and people could express their views ... As a result, some decisions came to light when wise men, people of good sense and judgment, and counsellors in the society were given the chance to express their well-respected views ...

In the present time and with life becoming increasingly complicated and interests entangled, the need for dialogue, discussion, and exchange of advice has, as a result, also increased. It has become a hallmark of nations' progress and development to the extent that there is a wide spread of advice and ideas bureaus like the spread of fire in straw. It has become difficult for someone who does a job that has a connection with others' interests to take a unilateral decision ...

In spite of this importance of dialogue, some people (unfortunately) have abused their right of discussion and confused the logical constructive debate with Byzantine debate which may lead to a departure from good manners to the exchange of accusations, insults, and swearing. Therefore, neither the debate has become a debate nor the views have become viewpoints ... Whoever wants to see examples of this can watch the debate programmes in the Arab media to see and listen to what takes place between the debaters and how the debate is run ... !!

This is a grave mistake and a failure on the part of the programme presenter. There are many debate programmes whose presenters are very wise and calm and have been well-known for discussing serious topical matters of great value to the world. Those presenters have run debates with prominent figures, scientists, thinkers, and world politicians.

Therefore, through the media we can make the art of balanced, fruitful, and objective debate deep-rooted in the Arab spectator.

Example 2:

كثير هم أولئك الذين ينظرون إلى الإنفاق التسويقي على انه هدر للاموال ورفع للتكاليف . وتمشياً مع هذا الطرح الذي لا يخلو من عدم الدقة ، فإننا نطرح السؤال الذي يعكس هذا التوجه بصورة أخرى وهو : كيف يتم تحقيق العائد المطلوب من الإنفاق التسويقي والحصول على أفضل عائد من ذلك الإستثمار ؟

في البداية لابد أن نعلم أن الإنفاق التسويقي ليس فقط ما يُنفق على الإعلان كما قد يتبادر الى كثير من الأذهان وخاصة الذين يرون أنه هدر للأموال ، وذلك لأن نظرتهم لم تكن متكاملة من البداية مما جعلهم يضعون هذا الإفتراض غير الدقيق .
. وإذا نظرنا إلى أعداد السكان خاصة في البلدان النامية نجدها في ازدياد مطرد مما يؤدي بطبيعة الحال إلى زيادة عدد من المستهلكين بشكل كبير ومتسارع وهذا عامل إيجابي أو على أقل تقدير يُفترض أن يؤدي إلى تحسين وجهة النظر السابقة عن الإنفاق التسويقي .
وحتى يتحقق ذلك بشكل عملي فإن هناك مجموعة من الأسئلة التي يجب الإجابة عليها للوصول إلى أفضل النتائج . وهناك أسئلة كثيرة ومتعلقة بجوانب عدة من جوانب التسويق . . والتي من خلال الإجابة عليها يمكن أن تتطابق إلى بقية القائمة من أسئلة حول الجوانب الأخرى للتسويق .
أنًّ الإجابة على مثل هذه الأسئلة هي البداية الصحيحة والحقيقية للتعرف على السوق وعلى المستهلكين وعلى الوسائل المناسبة للإتصال بالمستهلكين وغيرها من العوامل التي هي الأساس في العملية الإقتصادية للإنفاق التسويقي خاصة وأننا ننفق على جانب من جوانب التسويق دون أي دراسة أو تساؤل عن هذا الإنفاق ولمن تم توجيهه أو كيف تم هذا الإنفاق ثم نتذمر بعد ذلك .
(الرياض :ص ٣٢ الإثنين ٦ مارس ٢٠٠٠)

There are so many of those who look at marketing expenditure as a waste of money and increase in costs. In line with this viewpoint which is far from accurate, we ask the question that reflects this approach from a different way which is: How could the required result from marketing expenditure be achieved and how could we get the best result from this investment?

First, we need to learn that marketing expenditure is not only what is spent on advertising as it is understood by a lot of people especially those who see it as a total waste of money. This is because their opinion is incomplete from the beginning and that is what has made them put forward such an inaccurate assumption ...

If we look at the number of population especially in the developing countries, we find it increasing steadily which has naturally led to a consistent and considerable increase in the number of customers which is a positive factor or at least it will lead to an improvement in the previous point of view about marketing expenditure.

For that to take place in a practical way, there are some questions which need to be answered in order to arrive at the best results. There are many questions related to many aspects of marketing expenditure and which through their answers can match the rest of the list of questions about the other aspects of marketing.

The answer to these questions is the right and real beginning of knowing the market, the customers, the appropriate means of communication with customers, and other means which are the foundation of the economic process of marketing expenditure especially we spend on one aspect of marketing without any consideration or questioning this expenditure and to what it has been earmarked or how it has been done and then we complain after that.

Example 3:

النقطة التي تُثار دائماً في لقاءاتي مع المستشرقين هي أن الله سبحانه وتعالى أعدَّ حوراً عيناً في الجنة للرجال ولم يعد مثل ذلك للنساء . نقول لكل من يثير هذا الحديث أنك لاتفهم طبيعة الحياة . ذلك أن كرامة المرأة في أن يكون لها رجل واحد والمرأة المبتذلة هي التي يتعدد عليها الرجال . أما المرأة الحرة فقد يموت زوجها فترفض أن تتزوج حتى لايدخل عليها رجل آخر . وإذا كانت طبيعة خلق الله للمرأة هي أن كرامتها في ألاَّ يتعدد عليها الرجال فكيف يأتي الله سبحانه وتعالى في الجنة وهي دار النعيم ويجعلها دار إهانة للمرأة ؟ إن تعدد الرجال على المرأة الواحدة يخلق الأمراض الخبيثة فهل تريد من الله سبحانه وتعالى في الآخرة أن يهين كرامة المرأة وهل تعدد الرجال على المرأة الواحدة الذي هو نوع من الإهانة ونوع من الجلب للمرض نريد من الله أن يجعله في جنة كلها نعيم ؟ والمرأة الكريمة الشريفة تكره أن يتعدد عليها رجل آخر حتى بعد أن يموت زوجها وتلك هي الحكمة .

(محمد متولي الشعراوي – معجزة القرآن (الكتاب الثالث) ١٩٨٨ ص ٧٥)

The point that is always raised during my meetings with the Orientalists is that God prepared in Heaven wives with beautiful, big and lustrous eyes for men but He did not prepare something like that for women. We say to whoever raises this claim that you do not understand the very nature of life. This is because woman's dignity lies in the fact that she has one man while the debased woman is the one who has multitude of men. The husband of a noble woman may die but she refuses to re-marry so that she does not sleep with another man. If the nature of God's creation of woman is that her dignity lies in avoiding her many husbands, how then God makes Heaven, which is the place of blessing, a place of humiliation for the woman. The multitude of men for one woman creates malignant diseases. Do we want from God to make the multitude of men for one woman which is a kind of insult and a source of disease as part of Heaven which is all blessing. The noble respectable woman hates to have another man even when her husband dies and this is the wisdom.

Example 4:

لو كان الاسلام صالحا لكل عصر – كما يقول دعاته – لما أباح الرق ؟! وإن إباحة الرق لدليل قاطع على أن الاسلام قد جاء لفترة محددة ، وأنه أدى مهمته وأصبح في ذمة التأريخ !

وأن الشباب المسلم لتساوره الشكوك ! كيف أباح الاسلام الرق ؟
هذا الدين الذي لاشك في نزوله من عند الله كيف أبا الرق ؟ أو يريد الله للناس أن ينقسموا أبدا الى سادة وعبيد !
وإن الشباب المؤمن ليعلم أن الاسلام دين الحق ، ولكنه كإبراهيم : "قال : أولم تؤمن ؟ قال بلى ، ولكن ليطمئن قلبي !" . أما الشباب الذي أفسد الاستعمار عقله وعقائده فإنه لايتلبث حتي يتبين حقيقة الأمر . وأما الشيوعيون خاصة فأصحاب دعاوي مزيفة يتلقونها من سادتهم هناك . نحن ننظر اليوم الى الرق في ظروف القرن العشرين وننظر اليه في ضوء الشناعات التي ارتكبت في عالم النخاسة والمعاملة الوحشية البشعة التي سجلها التأريخ في العالم الروماني خاصة فنستفظع الرق ولا تطيق مشاعرنا أن يكون هذا اللون من المعاملة أمراً مشروعاً يقره دين أو نظام . كان الرقيق في عُرف الرومان "شيئاً" لا بشراً . . أشياء ليس لها كيان البشر ولا حقوق البشر . ثم جاء الاسلام ليرد لهؤلاء البشر إنسانيتهم . جاء ليقول للسادة عن الرقيق : "بعضكم من بعض" ويقول لهم الرسول : "من قتل عبده قتلناه ، ومن جدع عبده جدعناه" . جاء الاسلام ليقرر وحدة الاصل والمنشأ والمصير كما قال النبي : "أنتم بنوا آدم وآدم من تراب" . وأنه لافضل لسيد على عبد لمجرد أن هذا سيد وهذا عبد وإنما الفضل للتقوى . جاء ليقرر أن العلاقة بين السادة والرقيق ليست علاقة الاستعلاء والاستعباد أو التحقير وإنما هي علاقة القربى والأخوة . فالسادة "أهل" الجارية يستأذنون في زواجها : "فمن ما ملكت أيمانكم من فتياتكم المؤمنات . . بعضكم من بعض فانكحوهن بأذن أهلهن وآتوهن أجورهن بالمعروف" . لهذا لم يعد الرقيق "شيئاً" وإنما صار بشراً وأصبح الرقيق كائناً إنسانياً له كرامة يحميها القانون ولا يجوز الإعتداء عليها بالقول ولا بالفعل .
(محمد قطب – شبهات حول الاسلام : ١٩٩٥ ص ٣٠)

If Islam is suitable for each age – as its supporters say – why does it allow slavery? The authorization of slavery is hard evidence that Islam came for a specific period of time and that it fulfilled its mission and became something of the past. The Muslim youths have this doubt in their mind! How could Islam allow slavery? This religion which undoubtedly was revealed by God, why did it allow slavery? Does God want people to divide into masters and slaves?!
Young believers know very well that Islam is the religion of truth but like Abraham who said: "He (God) said: 'don't you believe, then?'. He (Abraham) said: 'Yea! but to satisfy my own understanding.'"(Qur'an 2:260). As for the youths whose minds and beliefs are spoiled by colonialism, they will soon realize the reality. As for the communists, in particular, they have false propaganda which they receive from their masters there. We look today at slavery from the twentieth century's perspective and in the light of the repulsiveness which was committed against the slave trade and the brutal repugnant treatment recorded by history especially during the Romans. Therefore, we are disgusted at slavery and our feelings cannot bear that such a kind of treatment be legal and permitted by any religion or system. The slave according to the Roman culture was "a thing" not human. Things which

neither had any human identity nor any human rights. Then Islam came to restore to those humans their humanity. It came to tell the masters about their slaves: "You are members, one of another" (Qur'an 3:195) and the Prophet said to them: "Whoever kills his slave, we shall kill him, and whoever mutilates a slave, we shall mutilate him". Islam came to determine the unity of origin and fate as the Prophet said: "You are the sons of Adam and Adam is from dust", and that there is no preference of a master over a slave just because the former is a master and the latter is a slave but preference is decided by piety. It came to determine that the relationship between the masters and the slaves was not a relationship of superiority, slavery or humiliation but it was a relationship of kinship and brotherhood. The masters who are the "family" of the female slave take her permission for marriage: "(To wed) believing girls from among those whom your right hands possess ... You are from one another. Wed them with the leave of their owners, and give them their dowers, according to what is reasonable" (Qur'an 4:25). Thus, the slave was not "a thing" but he/she became a human being. The male/female slave became a human creature with dignity which was protected by the (Islamic) law and no one could abuse it neither by words nor by deed.

Practical Exercises

تطبيقات

1. Specify the type of the following texts and discuss their major stylistic hallmarks:

١. واتجه الطبيب إلى الفراش فوضع عليه حقيبته ، وراح يفحص الراقدة ، أزاح جفنها محدقاً الى عينيها ، وجس النبض ، ثم أخرج من حقيبته السماعة وألصقها بالصدر فوق القلب ، ثم استمع إلى دقاته ، ثم أعادها الى الحقيبة وأغلقها ، وبسط فوقها ورقة وكتب على عجل بعض الكلمات وهو يقول : هذه الحقن لازمة . .

٢. السحالي نوع من الزواحف لها جسم جاف مغطى بالقشور ، ولها أطراف تساعدها على الحركة السريعة ، وتضع بيضاً ذا قشرة متينة لحماية الجنين بداخله وتتغذى السحالي بصفة عامة على الحشرات ولكن أعداداً منها تتغذى على النباتات . والسحالي ليست سامة فيما عدا نوعين فقط هما : وحش جيلا والسحلية المكسيكية ذات الخرز . وتختلف السحالي عن الثعابين بعض الإختلاف فللسحالي زوج من الأرجل وفتحتي أذن خارجيتان وأجفان متحركة ، كل هذه أشياء ليست عند الثعابين .

٣. دار اليمامة للبحث والترجمة والنشر

الرياض – المملكة العربية السعودية

من أهدافها :

– أُنشئت هذه الدار لنشر – ما تستطيع نشره – مما يتعلق ببلاد العرب من مؤلفات مما قد يكشف عن بعض النواحي الخفية من تأريخ تلك البلاد أو جغرافيتها أو أدبها أو تراثها الفكري .

– ترجمة بعض المؤلفات التي لها صلة بالجزيرة مما قد يُلقي ضوءاً على جانب مجهول يتعلق بها ، من رحلات أو دراسات .

– الإسهام بقدر الإمكان بنشر مؤلفات أبناء البلاد مما يضيف الى أدبنا أو ثقافتنا العربية جديداً .

وبالإضافة الى ما تقدم : تقوم الدار :

– بالإشراف على طبع ما يُراد طبعه والقيام بتصحيحه وفق رغبة صاحبه مما يتفق مع أهداف الدار – من كافة المطبوعات .

٤. الرفع السليم

– إفحص حجم المادة التي تود رفعها

– يجب أن تقوم في كل عملية رفع على إبقاء الرُكَب محنية والظهر مستقيماً

– أرفع بساقيك لا بظهرك

٥. تُعد العلاقة الوطيدة بين الأستاذ والطالب إحدى ركائز نجاح التعليم الجامعي ،

ولذلك يحرص القائمون على أمر التعليم في معظم بلاد العالم على دعم هذه العلاقة والعمل على تقوية الجسور وإشاعة روح الحب المتبادل بين الأستاذ وطالبه إيماناً منهم بأن إحياء هذه العلاقة إنما هو تدعيم حقيقي للتعليم الجامعي ولذلك نجد أن جامعات العالم إهتمت بالأخذ بنظام الأسر والعمل بروح الفريق .
ويعني هذا النظام أن يختار مجموعة من طلاب الكلية ينتمون الى مستويات مختلفة أحد الأساتذة ليكون رائداً لأسرة ذات إسم معين يتفق عليه من الطرفين .
كما يختار الجميع أحد الطلاب كأخ أكبر لهذه الأسرة .
ويمكن عن طريق نظام الأسر أن يكتسب الطلاب خبرات الأستاذ الجامعي التربوية والعلمية بما يصقل شخصيتهم وينمي المجالات المعرفية لديهم . كما يساهم كذلك في تكوين روح شابة لدى الطلاب تتسم بالحيوية وتتصف بالإيثار وتغليب العام على الخاص في كل الظروف . كما أن أسلوب محاكات النماذج يكسب الطلاب المهارات التي يحتاجها سوق العمل اليوم من قدرة على تحديد المشاكل وبناء الرأي والإختيار بين البدائل ودراسة الأولويات ويساعد في تدعيم قدراتهم البحثية وقدرتهم على التفاعل واتخاذ القرار والعمل بروح الفريق .

٦. ريكولا
تُلطِّف . . .
ريكولا
تُنعش . . .
ريكولا
تُخفِّف . . .
من إلتهاب الحلق ومن حدة نزلات البرد
متوفرة لدى الصيدليات والسوبرماركيت
تذوَّقوا ريكولا السويسرية بالأعشاب الطبيعية فهي تُنعش الفم وتهدىء الحنجرة والحلق واستمتعوا بطعمها الرائع
متوفرة بعدة نكهات طبيعية

٧. ظهر هذا الكتاب التربوي الهام برعاية المنظمة العربية للتربية والثقافة والعلوم في عام ١٩٨٧م . وهو ترجمة لكتاب كان قد أصدره المعهد الدولي للتخطيط التربوي ضمن سلسلة (الفكر التربوي العالمي) . ويتضمن الكتاب عدة دراسات ومقالات متفرقة بأقلام خبراء تربويين عالميين تتناول أحوال التربية والتعليم وسبل تطويرها في المديين القريب والبعيد . ويبين الكتاب أن المناهج الحالية في كثير من دول العالم وبخاصة النامية منها غير ملائمة وتعاني من القصور في التدريب المهني ومن عدم القدرة على اللحاق بالتطور العلمي والتقني والثقافي . ويرى الكتاب أن التنبؤ بمستقبل التربية أصعب من التنبؤ بالمجالات الأخرى نظراً لأن تطور التربية يرتبط إرتباطاً وثيقاً بالتطورات الأخرى السياسية منها والإقتصادية والإجتماعية والثقافية وغيرها .

٨. بدعوة من قسم التأريخ جامعة الرياض تم عقد الندوة العالمية الأولى لدراسة مصادر تأريخ الجزيرة . وقد هُيىء لهذه الندوة منذ أمد ليس بقريب حيث تم

تشكيل إثنتي عشرة لجنة كل لجنة منها أخذت على عاتقها جانباً من جوانب العمل المتعدد . ومن أهم هذه اللجان هي اللجنة التأسيسية واللجنة التنفيذية واللجنة العلمية ولجنة التأريخ . قام أعضاء اللجنة التأسيسية بزيارة لمعظم الجامعات العربية والأجنبية ووجهوا الدعوات بصورة مباشرة الى ذوي الإختصاص في تلك الجامعات . إفتُتحت الندوة في الساعة السابعة والنصف من مساء يوم الجمعة المصادف ٢٢ نيسان ١٩٧٧ برعاية السيد وزير التعليم العالي والبحث العلمي في قاعة المحاضرات العامة .

٩. الأخ/ حسين محمد أبو سيف ش/ت (٥٣٨٧)
بعد التحية . . .
بالإشارة إلى طلبكم المتعلق بشراء جهاز حاسب آلي لغرض استعماله أثناء الدراسة ، نأمل وعلى وجه السرعة تقديم تعهد كتابي بالعربية من طرفكم موجه إلى إدارة التدريب والتطوير تتعهد فيه بإعادة جهاز الحاسوب إلى إدارة التدريب بعد انتهاء البرنامج التدريبي وذلك حتى نتمكن من اتخاذ الإجراءات اللازمة بشأن اعتماد تغطية نفقات شراء الحاسوب .

والسلام عليكم ورحمة الله وبركاته

عبدالفتاح محمد شويعر
مدير التدريب والتطوير

١٠. المؤسسة العربية للتجارة والملاحة
(ذات مسؤولية محدودة)

شكر وتقدير
بمناسبة انتهاء عقد السيد/ صبر عبد الهادي صبر مدير عام تجارة الجملة بالقسم التجاري فإن الإدارة تقدم له خالص الشكر تقديراً لما قدمه من خدمات للمؤسسة طوال فترة عمله ونتمنى له التوفيق .
ولإنهاء أي معاملات أو متعلقات نأمل الإتصال بالإدارة قبل ١٩٩٩/١٢/٣١م بعمارة الجوهر طريق المدينة البغدادية تلفون : ٦٤٢٢٨.٨ جدة

١١. كان المماليك أفراداً من مناطق مختلفة . وكثير منهم من وسط آسيا . وقد اتخذ الملك الصالح أيوب فرقاً منهم في جيشه ، وكان لهم جهد بارز في الإنتصار على لويس التاسع واتباعه في المنصورة . ولما حضر توران شاه إلى مصر – بعد وفاة أبيه الملك الصالح – تسلَّم حُكم البلاد . لكنه أساء معاملة المماليك ، فقتلوه عام ٦٤٨ هـ . وأصبحت مقاليد الأمور في أيديهم . ويُعد ذلك بمثابة إنتهاء الدولة الأيوبية في مصر وقيام دولة المماليك مكانها . وكان أول حاكم من المماليك عز الدين أيبك الذي تزوج شجر الدر بعد وفاة زوجها الملك الصالح أيوب .

2. Write a text of 200 words as:

(i) a news report on an incident you have witnessed (ii) a story (iii) an informal letter to your friend (iv) instructions for decorating a house (v) a description of a party (vi) a book review (vii) a memoir of someone you know (viii) a thorough-argument on smoking.

3. Write an advertisement text of 30 words for each of the following items:

(i) washing powder (ii) car (iii) British Airways (iv) British Rail (v) mineral water.

Chapter Five
Rhetorical Description of Arabic
الوصفُ البلاغي للغةِ العربية

5.1 Introduction

Tropes and figures of speech are stylistically decorative building elements that can be employed to achieve an effective and sublime style. As we have seen in chapter four, the use of figurative expressions varies from one text type to another. The most fertile soil for figurative elements is fiction. However, we do encounter some figurative words in other text types, but to a lesser degree. The list of tropes and figures of speech provided in this chapter is of great stylistic value to the language user of Arabic. Due to the fact that Arabic and English are linguistically and culturally incongruous languages, the translation of some figures of speech may not reflect their real figurative and connotative value in Arabic.

5.2 Figures of Speech and Tropes الصور البلاغيّة والمجاز

The following is a list of the most commonly used tropes and figures of speech in Arabic as well as those that can be stylistically useful and effective.

Alliteration: المجانسة الإستهلالية

This is the repetition of the same initial letter, whether a consonant or a vowel, in successive words within a sentence or phrase, as in:

بات بدر بدون طعام – Badr slept without food.

where alliteration is achieved through the repeated initial letter (بـ) in the words (بات بدر بدون)

إستقبل أيمن أحد أصدقائه – Aymen received one of his friends.

Antithesis (Chiasmus): الطباق (التصالب)

This is when the structure of the sentence is converted in the second part of the sentence. Antithesis also takes place when the meaning of the first part is reversed in the second part, as in:

عندما يتعب الجسد ينشط الذهن . جسدي في حالة إرهاق وذهني في ذروة النشاط .

(حنا مينا – حكاية بحّار : ١٩٩١ ص ٣١٨)

When the body is tired, the mind is active. My body is in a state of exhaustion, and my mind is at the peak of activity,

where (يتعب الجسد - the body is tired) is the opposite of (ينشط الذهن - the mind is active), and (في حالة إرهاق - in a state of exhaustion) is the opposite of (في ذروة النشاط - at the peak of activity).

الواقع نوع من الحلم ، والحلم نوع من الواقع .
(نجيب محفوظ – دنيا الله ص ١٩٦)

Reality is a form of a dream, and a dream is a form of reality.

Assonance: التجانُس الصوتي

This is the repetition of the same sounds at word final position. Assonance can achieve sound patterning through partial rhyme, as in:

فقد كانت أُماً ضعيفة . . ضعيفة في فقرها ، ضعيفة في وحدتها ، ضعيفة في حيرتها مع الأقدار . .
(إحسان عبدالقدوس – أنا حرة : ١٩٧٧ ص ٢٧)

She was a weak mother ... weak in her poverty ... weak in her loneliness ... weak in her confusion with fate ...

Assonance is represented by the sound (ـها) at the end of the words (حيرتها ، وحدتها ، فقرها).

فلقد أعطى تيمور خالص حبه ووجدانه ووهب للقصة بالذات كل جهوده وصحته وقراءاته وكتاباته .
(مجلة العربي : ص ٤٠ العدد ١٨٣ فبراير (شباط) ١٩٧٤)

Taymor gave his genuine love and sentiment and donated to the novel in particular all his effort, health, reading, and writing.

Assonance is represented by the sound (ـه / ه) at the end of the words (كتاباته ، قراءاته ، صحته ، جهوده ، وجدانه ، حبه).

Asyndeton: الفصل

Asyndeton is the lack of conjunctions inter-sententially, as in:

إضطربت سلطات المدينة . إستدعت مخاتير الأحياء . هددت بإعدام "الخارجين على القانون" . أعطت الأوامر بإطلاق الرصاص فوراً على من يحوم حول الميناء . جنَّ جنون المستشار الفرنسي . ربط بين ما يجري في المدينة والحركات الثورية في المدن الأخرى . أنزل الجنود . سيَّر دوريات مسلحة . قام البوليس بغارات على الأحياء وبخاصة على حينا. إعتقل بعضهم . قتل آخرون ، واختفى الوالد نهائياً .
(حنا مينا – حكاية بحّار : ١٩٩١ ص ٢٧١-٢٧٢)

The city authorities were confused. They called the neighbourhood chiefs. They threatened to execute "those who do not abide by the law". They gave orders to shoot immediately every one who comes near the port. The French counsellor became crazy. He related what is going on in the city to the revolutionary movements in other cities. He deployed soldiers. He marched armed patrols. The police raided the neighbourhoods especially Hina. They arrested some. They killed others. And my father disappeared.

أسعد ما في اليوم هو هذا الوقت من الليل . إنتهت متاعب الواجبات . إستقر كل شيء في موضعه على أحسن حال . حتى المطبخ بات أنيقاً نظيفاً كأنه معروض للبيع . ألخادمة آوت إلى غرفتها لتنام . لم يبق إلا جلسة مريحة طويلة يبهجها الحب العائلي حول الراديو المردد لشتى المسرات .
(نجيب محفوظ – دنيا الله : ١٩٧٢ ص٦٩)

The best time of the day is this time of the night. The hard work of duties has finished. Every thing has settled very well in its place. Even the kitchen has become tidy and clean as if it was for sale. The maid went to her room to sleep. Nothing is needed except a long comfortable gathering surrounded by family love around the radio that broadcasts joy.

Epithet: النعت

Epithets are descriptive words; in grammar, however, these words are referred to as adjectives, as in:

كانوا يُسمونه الصادقُ الأمين – They used to call him the truthful and the trustworthy.

The epithets are (صادق - truthful) and (أمين - trustworthy).

طه حسين كاتب عبقري – Taha Hussein is a writer of genius.

The epithet is (عبقري - genius).

فامتعضت تفيدة وتوردّ وجهها النحيل الشاحب العاطل من الجمال .
(نجيب محفوظ – دنيا الله : ١٩٧٢ ص ٢٤)

Tafidah became annoyed and her hollow, pale, and void of beauty face reddened.

The epithets are (نحيل - hollow), (شاحب - pale), and (عاطل - void of).

Epizeuxis: التوكيد (التكرار التوكيدي)

Epizeuxis is the repetition of the same word or words in successive sentences, as in:

هبطت الطائرة ، هبطت الطائرة – The aeroplane has landed, the aeroplane has landed.

فقد كانت أُماً ضعيفة . . ضعيفة في فقرها ، ضعيفة في وحدتها ، ضعيفة في حيرتها مع الأقدار . .
(إحسان عبد القدوس – أنا حرة : ١٩٧٢ ص ٢٧)

She was a weak mother ... weak in her poverty ... weak in her loneliness ... weak in her confusion with fate ...

Euphemism: التهوين

Euphemism is the use of a pleasant expression instead of an unpleasant, distasteful, or taboo one.

Examples:

The expressions (إنتقل الى رحمة الله - he moved to the mercy of God; إنتقل الى جوار ربه - he moved next to his Lord) are euphemisms for (مات - to die)
The expressions (بيت الأدب - the place of manners, دورة مياه - water-closet) are euphemisms for (المرحاض - the toilet).
The expression (البلدان النامية - the developing countries) is a euphemism for (البلدان الفقيرة أو المتخلفة - poor or underdeveloped countries).
The words (بصير - endowed with eyesight) and (كفيف - the one who shades his eyes with his hands) are euphemisms for (أعمى - blind).
The expression (كبت الطائرة - the aircraft stumbled) is the euphemism of (أسقط العدو الطائرة - the aircraft has been shot down (by enemy fire)).

Head-Tail/Tail-Head: رد العجز على الصدر / رد الصدر على العجز

This is when the first lexical item (Head) in a sentence is repeated at the end (Tail) of the following sentence, or when the last lexical item (Tail) of the first sentence is repeated as an initial word (Head) in the second sentence, as in:

أكاد أرى صورتها على الجدران . . وأحس بالخوف . خوف يستبد بي الى حد الرعب . .
(إحسان عبد القدوس – لا أنام ص ٣٢)

I almost see her picture on the wall . . and I feel afraid. Fear dominates me to the degree of horror.

where the word (خوف - fear) is the Tail and the word (خوف - fear) is the Head.

أنه يقف أمام جريمة بلا شك . والجريمة لا توجد إلا بمجرم . والمجرم لا يُستدل عليه

إلا بأثر . . فالقاتل جاء من الباب ، ومن الباب خرج .
(نجيب محفوظ – دنيا الله : ١٩٧٢ ص ٩٩)

He is undoubtedly standing in front of a crime. The crime does not take place without a criminal. The criminal cannot be found without a mark. The murderer came in through the door, and through the door he left.

The Tails are (مجرم - criminal) and (مجرم) whose Heads are (من الباب - through the door) and (من الباب) respectively.

Hyperbole: المبالغة

Hyperbole means exaggeration which has an emotive function, as in:

طه حسين ، هذا الأديب العبقري الذي شقَّ طريقه بين الصخور وواجه العواصف في إباء وما زادته الشدائد إلا إستمساكاً بما يؤمن به ويدعو إليه – هذا الأديب تلقّى مئات الرسائل . . .
(مجلة العربي : ص ٣٦ العدد ٢١٦ نوفمبر (تشرين الثاني) ١٩٧٦)

Taha Hussein, this writer of genius who fought his way through rocks, faced the gales with pride, and hardship made his belief firmer in what he believed in and called for, this writer received hundreds of letters ...

where we find hyperbole expressions (شق طريقه بين الصخور - he fought his way through rocks) and (واجه العواصف في إباء - he faced gales with pride).

العربيةُ بحر خضم – Arabic is a vast sea.
قلتُ لكَ سبعين مرّة لا تُؤخر عملك – I told you seventy times not to delay your work.
سأقتُلك إذا أخبرتهم بذلك – I'll kill you if you tell them that.

Irony: السخرية

Irony expresses covert contempt and rebuke. It is a way of speech in which we say words which, in actual fact, mean the opposite of our intended meaning; for instance, you say to a miser or greedy person (ما أكرمك - what a generous person you are) but in fact your intended meaning is (ما أبخلك - how miserly you are!).

Therefore, irony is used as an indirect satire, a rebuke, or scorn and contempt.

نام الطلاب خلال محاضرته الممتعة – Students fell asleep during his interesting lecture.

The word (ممتعة - interesting) is used as an irony but the intended meaning of the word is the opposite which is (مُملة - boring).

Litotes: الإثبات بالنفي

Litotes takes place when we negate an expression in order to provide the opposite meaning, as in:

الجدل ليس مُجدياً – Argumentation is not advantageous.
ليست العربية صعبة – Arabic is not difficult.
وقد هُيىء لهذه الندوة منذ أمد ليس بقريب حيث تم تشكيل إثنتي عشرة لجنة – The preparation for this symposium has not been going on recently where twelve committees have been established.

Litotes is expressed by the expressions (ليس مجديا), (ليست صعبة), and (ليس بقريب) whose actual meanings are (ضار), (سهلة), and (بعيد) respectively.

Metaphor: الإستعارة

Metaphor is based on similitude, i.e., there is a relationship between metaphor and simile. In metaphor, however, we do not use the particles (كـ / مثل), as in:

إنَّ الميناء هو الرئة لأي قُطر من الأقطار ، فهو الذي تتنفَّس منه الدولة بالصادرات والواردات .
(مجلة العربي : ص ٨٣ العدد ٢١٦ نوفمبر (تشرين الثاني) ١٩٧٦)

The port is the lung for any country through which the country breathes its exports and imports.

The metaphors are represented by the words (الرئة - the lung, تتنفس - breathe).

إنَّ القرن الواحد والعشرين يطرق أبوابنا – The twenty-first century is knocking at our doors.
The metaphor is represented by the word (يطرق - knock at).

ويهجم الليل ويعُم الظلام ، ويداعبُ النعاس عينيَّ فأغفو ، ولا أدري كم مضى من الوقت .
(مجلة العربي : ص ٨٨ العدد ٣٦٨ يوليو (تموز) ١٩٨٩)

The night attacks and darkness prevails. Sleepiness fondles my eyes and then I fall asleep. I do not know how much time elapsed.

The metaphors are represented by the words (يهجم - to attack) and (يداعب - to fondle).

كنا أمام دكان سعيد والليل يزحف حثيثاً . .
(الطيب صالح – ضو البيت ١٩٩٧ ص ٩)

We were in front of Said's shop and the night was crawling fast.

The metaphor is represented by the word (يزحف - crawl).

وكان أول المتكلمين شاباً نزقاً يعمل بائعاً لملابس نسائية ، وقد صاح بحماسة : "لنُحارب" . فوثبت عليه تواً نظرات الإزدراء . .
(زكريا تامر – الرعد ١٩٧٨ ص ٣٢)

The first one to speak was a heedless young man selling women's clothes who shouted with enthusiasm: "let us fight". Then, looks of contempt pounced upon him . . .

The metaphor is represented by the word (وثب – to pounce).

Metonymy: الكناية

Metonymy takes place when we replace an expression by another expression like (الصُحُف – newspapers) which is replaced by the metonymy word (الصحافة – the media). Metonymy expressions are like:

(ضيوف الرحمن – guests of the Most Gracious) is the metonymy of (حُجَّاج – pilgrims).
(بنت عدنان – Adnan's daughter) is the metonymy of (اللغة العربية – Arabic language).
(دار السلام – the house of peace, بلد الرشيد – Al-Rashid's country) are the metonymy of (بغداد – Baghdad).
(مدينة الضباب – the city of fog) is the metonymy of (لندن – London).
(سفينة الصحراء – the ship of the desert) is the metonymy of (جمل – camel).
(كبير القلب – big hearted) is the metonymy of (رؤوف – kind).
(نسور الجو – eagles of the sky) is the metonymy of (طيَّار عسكري – aircraft pilot).

Onomatopoeia: المُحاكات الصوتية

Onomatopoeia refers to the symbolism of sounds and the verbalization of noises. Onomatopoeic expressions in Arabic are like (شخَّاط – matches), (صاروخ – missile), (قهقهة – to laugh boisterously, a loud burst of laughter), (ولولة المرأة – wailing or lamenting of a woman), (نحيب المرأة – loud weeping of a woman), (خرير الماء – ripple of water), (حفيف الشجر – the rustling of leaves), (هديج البحر – the crashing of waves), (صهيل الخيل / الفرس – neighing of horses), (رغاء الجمل – the noise of the camel), (نباح الكلب – barking of dog), (عواء الذئب – howling of a wolf), (مواء القط – mewing of a cat), (خوار البقر – the mooing of the cow), (ثُغاء الشاة – the bleating of sheep), (دوي المدافع – the bang of guns), (دقات الساعة – the ticking of the clock), (رنين الجرس – the ringing of the bell), (تغريد الطيور – the twittering of birds).

Oxymoron: الإرداف الخُلفي

Oxymoron takes place when two contradictory expressions are placed next to each other, as in:

قلق دولي من تزايد حجم الإنتاج في أفغانستان
حقول الأفيون تتسع لتمويل حروب "الأخوة الأعداء"
(أنباء الجريمة (ملحق إسبوعي لصحيفة الأنباء الكويتية) : ص ١٢ في ١٩ اكتوبر (تشرين الأول) ١٩٩٦)

International Concern at the Increase in Output in Afghanistan
Aphion Fields Expand to Fund the Series of Wars Between the "Brother Enemies"

حاول أن يقنعنا بحقائق كاذبة – He tried to convince us with false facts.

بطأت سرعة التقدم الإقتصادي جراء سياسته المالية الخاطئة – The speed of economic progress slowed down due to his wrong financial policy.

سياسة حزب العمال مبنية على وعود كاذبة – The Labour policy is based on false promises.

بطأت سرعة القطار عندما اقتربنا من المحطة – The train's speed slowed down when we approached the station.

Oxymoron has taken place in the expressions (الأخوة الأعداء - brother enemies), (حقائق كاذبة - false facts), (وعود كاذبة - false promises) and (بطأت سرعة - the speed slowed down).

Parallelism: الموازنة (المماثلة)

This is when a phrase is parallel in grammatical structure and rhyme with another phrase, as in:

كل ساعة منها حصيلة تقنية فائقة ومراقبة صارمة لمستوى الجودة .
(مجلة العربي : ص ٢ العدد ٢٣٦ يوليو (تموز) ١٩٧٨)

Every watch of theirs is the result of excellent technology and stringent observation to achieve excellence.

The parallelism is represented by the phrases (تقنية فائقة) and (مراقبة صارمة).

فوالده المرحوم أحمد تيمور باشا كان عالماً جليلاً وباحثاً أصيلاً .
(مجلة العربي : ص ٤٠ العدد ١٨٣ فبراير (شباط) ١٩٧٤)

His father the late Ahmad Taymor Basha was a great scholar and a genuine researcher.

The parallelism is represented by the phrases (عالماً جليلاً) and (باحثاً أصيلاً).

وحين الفجر صعد المؤذّن الى أعلى المئذنة في ليلٍ ساجٍ ، وبدرٍ ساطعٍ ، وسكونٍ مؤثرٍ .

(نجيب محفوظ – دنيا الله : ١٩٧٢ ص ٦٢)

At dawn, the caller to prayers went up the minaret in a dark night, shining crescent, and impressive tranquility.

The parallelism is represented by the phrases (ليلٍ ساجٍ), (بدرٍ ساطعٍ) and (سكونٍ مؤثرٍ).

Parenthesis: الإعتراض

Parenthesis is an extra word or phrase which is inserted within a sentence in order to provide an extra explanation and without it the sentence will still be complete, as in:

ورقيا في السُلّم ، وهو سُلّمٌ عالي الدرجات ، حتى لهث عبدالعظيم .

(نجيب محفوظ – دنيا الله : ١٩٧٢ ص ٢٥)

They took the steps, which are high steps, until Abdul-Athim was out of breath.

The parenthesis is represented by (وهو سلم عالي الدرجات - they are high steps). The main sentence is (ورقيا في السلم حتى لهث عبدالعظيم - They took the steps until Abdul-Athim was out of breath).

وكان الرئيس عرفات قد أشاد – خلال لقائه مساء أمس بالسفير المصري في تونس مخلص قطب – بدور مصر في دعم القضية الفلسطينية .

(الأهرام : ٢٧ يناير (كانون الثاني) ١٩٩٨ ص ١)

President Yasir Arafat praised - during his meeting last night with the Egyptian ambassador in Tunisia Mr Mukhlis Qutub - Egypt's role in supporting the Palestinian cause.

The parenthesis is represented by (خلال لقائه مساء . . . مخلص قطب - during his meeting . . Mukhlis Qutub). The main sentence is (وكان الرئيس عرفات قد أشاد بدور مصر في دعم القضية الفلسطينية - President Yasir Arafat praised Egypt's role in supporting the Palestinian cause).

ويبين الكتاب أن المناهج الحالية في كثير من دول العالم وبخاصة النامية منها غير ملائمة .

(مجلة القافلة : ص ١٤ المجلد ٣٨ العدد ٨ فبراير – مارس ١٩٩٠)

The book explains that the present curricula in many countries especially the developing ones are not appropriate.

The parenthesis is represented by (في كثير من دول العالم وبخاصة النامية منها - in many countries especially the developing ones). The main sentence is (ويبين الكتاب أن المناهج الحالية غير ملائمة - The book explains that the present curricula are not appropriate).

Personification: التشخيص

Personification takes place when we give the attributes of human beings to non-human, inanimate or abstract nouns, as in:

وقد فكَّر الصَّرار ثم ابتسم قائلاً "أنا سعيد جداً . . " وقال الصَّرار للنملة سأرقص وأغني ..

(إقرأ / الجزء الثاني – للصف الثاني الابتدائي : ١٩٨٦ ص ٥٨)

The cockroach thought for a while and said smiling "I am very happy ..."

where personification is represented in the words (فكر - to think), (ابتسم - to smile), (قائلا - saying), (أرقص - to dance) and (أغني - to dance).

في هذه اللحظة إنفجرت الحيوانات ضحكاً إذ أن يد المعتدي عليه مكسورة .

(سمر المزغمي – محاكمة ذئب : ٢٠٠٠ ص ٢)

In the meantime, the animals burst out laughing because the victim's hand was broken.

Also, in personification, we can find the animation of the inanimate, as in:

ضحك الصخر - The stones laughed.
بكت السماء - The sky wept.

Polyptoton: جِناسُ الإشتقاق

Polyptoton is the repetition of a word in different forms that are morphologically related to it, i.e., the repeated words are derived from the same root, as in:

سيخرج من السجن كل من لا يستحق السجن حقاً ولو فرغت السجون .

(نجيب محفوظ – دنيا الله : ١٩٧٢ ص ١٩٦)

Every one who does not indeed deserve to be in prison will leave prison even if prisons would be empty.

We have polyptoton between the word (يستحق - deserve) which is a verb and its derivative form (حق - rightly) which is a noun.

وكان حقاً يبتسم . إبتسامة جديدة . . لا نفاقاً ولا إستفزازاً ولا سُخريةً . . إبتسامةً صافية .
(نجيب محفوظ – دنيا الله : ١٩٧٢ ص ١٧٦)

Polyptoton is realized in this example between the word (يبتسم - to smile) which is a verb and its derivative forms (إبتسامة - a smile) and (إبتسامة - a smile) which are nouns.

Polysyndeton: الوصل البلاغي

Polysyndeton is the over-use of conjunctions inter-sententially, as in:

ولم تمض سوى لحظات حتى هيمن السكون ثانية على البيت ، فعاودت لميا الإستلقاء على السرير ، ولكنها نهضت بعد لحظات وأضاءت النور ، ووقفت أمام المرآة ، ونظرت الى وجهها مليا ثم ابتسمت وأطفأت النور ، وتمددت على السرير مستسلمة لنوم عميق ، وظل وجهها محتفظاً بالإبتسامة .
(زكريا تامر – الرعد ١٩٧٨ ص ١٠)

Only a few moments passed and quiet dominated the house. Lamia continued lying down on bed but she rose after a while and turned on the light and stood in front of the mirror and looked at her face for a long time and then she smiled and turned off the light and lay in bed and surrendered to fast sleep and her face preserved the smile.

ورفعته أمه بين يديها وجففت دموعه بشفتيها ، وأجلسته الى جانبها على فراشها وعزَّته بكلمات رقيقة ، ولكنه لم يسمع إليها ولم تنفرج شفتاه تلك الليلة . وهكذا اختُتِم ذلك اليوم الحزين .
(نجيب محفوظ – عبث الأقدار : ص ١٣٨)

His mother lifted him between her hands and dried his tears with her lips, and sat him by her side on her bed and offered her condolences to him with soft words, but he did not listen to her and his lips never opened that night. Thus that sad day was concluded.

Polysyndeton in the above examples is represented by the over-use of the additive conjunctive element (و).

Rhetorical Question: الإستفهام البلاغي

This is a question which does not require an answer because it stresses something that is already known to the reader/listener, as in:

ألم أحذِّرْكَ من ذلك مسبقاً ؟ – Haven't I warned you against it already?

شرحت هذه المسألة مراراً وتكراراً ، أليس كذلك ؟ – I explained this matter over and over again. Isn't it right?

Simile: التَّشبيه

Simile takes place when we compare two things in an imaginative or descriptive way using one of the comparison particles (كـ - like, as) or (مثل - like, as), as in:

وخرج من غرفته مندفعاً كالصاروخ المشتعل .
(إحسان عبدالقدوس – لاتطفيء الشمس .١٩٦٠ ص ٤٣٢)

And he left his room in a hurry like a burning missile,
where the simile is in (كالصاروخ - like a missile).

كلامكَ كالبرتقال السُكَّري
(نجيب محفوظ – أولاد حارتنا ١٩٦٧ ص ١١٩)

Your speech is like sweet oranges.

The simile is represented by the word (كالبرتقال - like oranges) through the particle (كـ).

Stress: التوكيد

The stress particles in Arabic are (إنَّ / أنَّ - certainly, surely, truly), (قد - definitely), and (لـ - to). The stress particles (إنَّ / أنَّ) are used before a noun or adjective to be stressed, the particle (قد) is used before a verb, and the stress particle (لـ) can be used before a noun or an epithet, as in:

إنَّ الأمرَ مُعقَّدٌ جداً – The matter is (certainly) very complicated.
جئتُ لأعتذر لك – I have (definitely) come to apologize to you.
إنه لغني أكثر مما تتوقعَ – He is (indeed) richer than you expect.
وقد إستنكرت البلدان العربية هذا القرار – The Arab countries have (definitely) condemned this resolution.

Synecdoche: المجاز المُرسَل

Synecdoche takes place when we mention a part of a person or thing that refers to the whole of the person or thing or vice versa, as in:

وقد تصدى المحامون لهذه الظاهرة وضموا صوتهم الى صوت الكثيرين الذين يطالبون بتشريع كويتي متشدد يحمي حقوق التأليف والإبداع .
(أنباء الجريمة : ص ١٢ في ١٩ أوكتوبر (تشرين الأول) ١٩٩٦)

Lawyers confronted this phenomenon and added their voice to the voice of many people who demanded a firm Kuwaiti legislation that could protect the rights of writing and creative ability.

The synecdoche words are (صوت/صوتهم - their voice/voice) which refer to one voice only since the word (صـــــوت) is used in the singular. This singular word refers to all the voices of the lawyers and the voices of other people.

أردت أن أنصحهم ولكن كلما أتكلم معهم يضعوا أصابعهم في آذانهم ويسخروا مني ..

I wanted to advise them but whenever I talked to them, they put their fingers in their ears and made fun of me.

جرح الطفل يده – The child cut his hand.

Synecdoche is represented by the words (أصـبـع - finger) and (يـد - hand) because only part and not the whole of the finger is put in the ear, and only part and not the whole hand is cut.

Zeugma: العبارة الجامعة

This is when a word is used in a special context with a meaning different from its normal meaning, as in:

أُحبُّ اللغة العربية – I love Arabic.

The word (يـحـب - to love) is a zeugma because it is normally used in other contexts such as man to woman or vice versa.

يتناول هذا الكتاب الدراسات الإسلوبية للغة العربية – This book eats (i.e., deals with) Arabic stylistics.

The word (يـتـنـاول - to eat) is a zeugma because it is normally used with food, as in (أتـنـاول عشائي في السادسة - I eat my supper at six).

أرجو أن لا تخوض في هذا الموضوع لأنه حسَّاس – Please do not wade in (i.e., talk about) this topic as it is sensitive.

The zeugma word is (خـــــاض) because it is normally used with water meaning (to wade).

Practical Exercises

تطبيقات

Underline and mention the type of tropes and figures of speech in the following sentences:

١. وكانت حفلة عرس عادية . . فبعد ما شكر العريس أهل العروس على جهودهم المادية والمعنوية ، أخرج صورة لزوجته مع عشيقها الذي كان من بين الحاظرين وقال : "عذراً على المضايقة" ومضى يفسخ زواجه الطّازج .
(الحياة : ٣ فبراير (شباط) ٢٠٠٠ ص ٢٤)

٢. وكنت في هذه الوحدة التي يتركني فيها أبي . . لا أنام . . أطوف بين الغرف كأني أهرب من غرفة الى غرفة ، وأحس في هربي بطنط صفية تلاحقني . . أكاد أرى صورتها على الجدران . . وأكاد أسمع خطواتها تتبع خطواتي . . إنها في كل مكان من البيت . . كانت تجلس هنا . . وكانت تأكل هنا . . وهنا كانت تشغل التريكو . .

٣. سمعنا همسته المدوية

٤. أنَّ زيارة حسني مبارك إلى بيروت كسرت عُزلة لبنان .
(العرب : ٢٤ فبراير (شباط) ٢٠٠٠ ص ١)

٥. فتح عينيه ، فتح عينيه

٦. تناولت المحادثات مشكلة الحدود واستئناف العلاقات الدبلوماسية .

٧. إنقضَّ المُخبرون على قهوة فؤاد ثم رجعوا إلى القسم .

٨. لقد اقتربت الإمتحانات ولهذا عليكم أنْ تدرسوا كثيراً وتلهوا قليلاً .

٩. وخنقتها العبرات ، فسكتت حتى انحسرت عنها موجة البكاء وقالت : . .

١٠. الناسُ . . وجوهُهُم شاحبة فيها غُضون وعُيونُهم ذابلة فيها شتاء .
(يوسف إدريس – أليس كذلك؟ ١٩٥٧)

١١. أخفق البيض ثم ضعه على النار

١٢. أعتقد أنَّ لها يداً في هذا الأمر

١٣. ومضى مُهرولاً يخوض ظلاماً دامساً

١٤. فؤاد وزينب صديقان لدودان

١٥. رغم الفتونة والجدعة لم تقبض يده على جنيه بالكامل إلا فيما ندر . لكنه لم يقتل . ضرب وسرق ولكنه لم يقتل . لم يقتل . لم يقتل وإن تكن ضربته قاتلة .
(نجيب محفوظ – دنيا الله : ١٩٧٢ ص ٨٨)

١٦. ويرى الكتاب أن التنبؤ بمستقبل التربية أصعب من التنبؤ بالمجالات الأخرى.
(مجلة القافلة : ص ١٤ المجلد ٣٨ عدد ٨ فبراير – مارس ١٩٩٠)

١٧. وبدأت الأم تغفو ثم تصحو منزعجة كلما سكت الصراخ.
(إحسان عبدالقدوس – أنا حرة : ١٩٧٧ ص ٢٧)

١٨. أخذ الوعيُ يلطمُني كقبضة شرطي.

١٩. وقال الضابط لنفسه أنَّ هذا البواب لا يستطيع أنْ يخنق دجاجة.

٢٠. دفتر توفير . . دفتر توفير وحياة ربنا.

٢١. ما أشبهه بصوت العسكري ! العسكري القديم بصوته الخشن.

٢٢. فقال الحاج مصطفى بعفوية عجيبة : "أقطع ذراعي إنْ طلع عليها الصبح !"

٢٣. تبيَّن أنَّ الجنون فنون وربما أنَّ الفنون جنون.

٢٤. أخذ الوضعُ بالتحسُّن

٢٥. طار فكر عبدالعظيم إلى إبنه

٢٦. هو الأبُ ، هو الأخُ ، هو الصديقُ ، هو المعوانُ ، هو كل شيء

٢٧. نسيتُ قواعد اللغة العربية

٢٨. بسم الله الرحمن الرحيم

٢٩. كان طه حسين بصيراً منذ صِغره

٣٠. سُدَّت في وجهي السُّبُل وطوَّقني اليأس

٣١. وكان عبد الله قد لعب دوراً في تحسين الأقتصاد وتخفيض الضرائب

٣٢. إنتقل مدرس الجغرافية الى رحمة الله

٣٤. وقال وهو يلتقط يدها ويضغط عليها : إن لقاءاتنا لا تحدد لنا مستقبل . . حتى ثقتنا في عواطفنا ليست هي المستقبل . . المستقبل هو الحياة التي نعيشها معاً . . أنتِ تعرفين الفارق الكبير بين حالتك وحالتي . . أنتِ من عائلة في منتهى الغنى وأناَ من عائلة ليست في منتهى الفقر ولكنها ليست غنية . .
(إحسان عبد القدوس – الحياة فوق الضباب : ١٩٨٤ ص ١١٦–١١٧)

٣٥. كان شلال الدموع ينهمر . . كان العمر كله يتلاشى . . مثلما كانت كل الآمال تذوب . . تذوب . . ثم يمحى أثرها.
(مجلة القافلة : ص ٣١ فبراير/مارس ١٩٩٧)

٣٦. قال عيسى لسلوى : في حياتنا سر يجب أن تعرفيه . .
وهما يجلسان في الفرندا المفعمة بعبير الورد والقرنفل . والمغيب يقترب نصف مسدل الجفنين ، والشمس تسحب أهدابها من هامات القصور ، والربيع يتنفس شباباً رائقاً . .

(نجيب محفوظ – السَّمان والخريف : ١٩٨٨ ص ٢٩)

٣٧. السحالي ليست سامة وعندها أشياء ليست عند الثعابين .

٣٨. بحثت عن الكتاب في كل المكتبات ولم أجده .

٣٩. تراميتم فقال الناسُ قومٌ
الى الخذلان أمرهمُ ترامى
(أحمد شوقي – الشوقيات : الجزء الأول ١٩٦٤ ص ٢٦٢)

٤٠. هذه الواقعة حفرتها الأيام في ذاكرتي ولم أنسها حتى الآن ، ومنذ ذلك الوقت عرفت معنى كلمة حشيش أو إفيون .
(أنباء الجريمة : ص ١٢ في ١٩ أوكتوبر (تشرين الأول) ١٩٩٦)

٤١. أنقذوا عقله وجسده وروحه
(مجلة العربي : ص ٣ العدد ٢٣٦ يوليو (تموز) ١٩٧٨)

٤٢. أشترينا خمسين رأس غنم

٤٣. رحل الفريق الأول محمد فوزي بطل حرب الإستنزاف يوم أمس بعد أن هزمه المرض .

٤٤. وعدت وزيرة الخارجية الأمريكية مادلين أولبرايت باتخاذ خطوات تؤدي الى الإفراج عن الأموال الإيرانية المجمدة منذ سقوط الشاه في ١٩٧٩ والتي تقدر ببلايين الدولارات .

Chapter Six
Stylistic Analysis of Texts
التحليل الإسلوبي للنُصوص

6.1 Introduction

This is a practical account of what we have discussed in the previous chapters. We have discussed the workings of Arabic which include the sentence structure in Arabic, the description of Arabic words, the cohesion network in Arabic, the various text types or styles which we encounter in Arabic, and the rhetorical hallmarks of Arabic. We now need to be familiar with the analysis of Arabic texts from a stylistic perspective by unearthing the major components that constitute the Arabic text. These textual elements are the hallmarks of Arabic style and vary from one style to another. In our stylistic analysis, we shall provide a checklist of textual features that can be applied to any text type or any style in Arabic. Our stylistic analysis is based on a number of features which aim at providing a systematic stylistic analysis. Our checklist of features includes: grammatical features, lexical features, cohesive features, textual features, and rhetorical features.

6.2 Checklist of Features قائمة المزايا

6.2.1 Grammatical Features مزايا نحوية

In our stylistic analysis of Arabic, we need to account for the various types of sentence structures employed in a given text. We need to see the sentence structure choices a given writer makes, i.e., whether the writer uses basic or derived sentences, verbal or nominal sentences, passive or periphrastic passive sentences, imperative or vocative sentences, negative or instructional sentences, compound or complex sentences, parenthetical or interrogative sentences. It is also important to see whether a text provides sentences that begin with other elements other than the verb such as adjuncts like (بسرعة - quickly, بهدوء - quietly), or like (على الشاطيء - on the beach, في الصباح - in the morning), or direct objects. We also need to look at the type of verbs employed in the text, i.e., whether the text is dominated by transitive verbs or intransitive verbs, adjectives or adverbs. Tense is also important to observe in our stylistic analysis to see whether the writer favours present, future or past tenses. We also need to look for the frequency of prepositions, conjunctions, demonstrative pronouns, or relative pronouns. It is also important to see the type of pronouns used, i.e., whether they are used in the first, second or third person, singular or plural. We also need to see whether the stress particles like (إنَّ / أنَّ) are employed frequently.

6.2.2 Lexical Features مزايا مُفرداتيَّة

In our analysis of the lexical features of a text, we need to investigate the occurrence of formal or informal words, emotive, comparative or descriptive words, words with connotative overtones, culture-specific words, words which reflect the writer's socio-political or religious beliefs, dialectal expressions, or specialized words. We also need to see whether semantic fields are used. The various types of general noun is also important to check to see whether abstract, concrete, human, non-human, animate or inanimate nouns occur more frequently than other types of general noun. We also need to see whether the writer employs ameliorative or pejorative expressions, adjectives or epithets and whether they are emotive or not. It is essential to investigate the semantic relations within the text by looking at the occurrence of colligations, synonyms, antonyms, hyponyms, polysemes, homonyms, acronyms, calques, loan words and neologisms. It is also useful to check the use of active/passive participle words and the use of the absolute object. In our analysis, we should also see whether the text is dominated by content words (open class words) or by the non-content words (closed class words) such as pronouns, conjunctions, prepositions.

6.2.3 Cohesive Features مزايا تماسُك النَّص

The checklist of cohesive hallmarks investigates the network of cohesion which we find intra-sententially and inter-sententially. We need to look at the different types of cohesion. We look for types of reference like personal, general, extended, demonstrative, comparative, anaphoric, and cataphoric reference. We need to see whether the writer uses nominal or verbal substitution, nominal or verbal ellipsis, and whether additive conjunction, adversative conjunction, and temporal conjunction are used in the text. It is important to see whether lexical cohesion through collocation or reiteration is employed in the text.

6.2.4 Textual Features مزايا نصيّة

In our stylistic analysis, we need to specify the macro textual hallmark of the text, i.e., the type of text or style used by the writer. It is important to differentiate between the various text types and see whether the text is expository or narrative, journalistic or non-fictional, instructional or descriptive. We also need to be familiar with the general theme of the text, i.e., what the text is all about.

6.2.5 Rhetorical Features مزايا بلاغيّة

Our checklist of rhetorical features includes the figures of speech and tropes used by the writer such as alliteration, chiasmus, epithets, head-tail/tail-head, hyperbole, irony, metaphor, metonymy, personification, polyptoton, simile, and zeugma.

6.3 Application of Stylistic Analysis تطبيق التحليل الإسلوبي

We shall apply the above checklist of features on the following text and try to provide a thorough account of stylistic features of this sample.

عندما يحل الصيف وتبدأ العطلات ، يأخذ الفراغ الذي يعاني منه الشباب العربي صبغة "رسمية" . ويمتليء الشارع العربي بألوف الألوف من الشباب التائه والحائر . . ماذا يفعلون لثلاثة أو أربعة أشهر قادمة ؟

السؤال لا يشغل الكثيرين من الذين يفترض أنهم يخططون ويفكرون لمستقبل هؤلاء الشباب ، لأن الحاح شواغل الحاضر يحجب فيما يبدو رؤية المستقبل ، لكن ذلك لا يؤجل المشكلة . وإنما يزيدها تعقيداً .

حقاً ، ماذا يفعل الشباب العربي طوال أشهر الصيف ؟

هم قلة أولئك الذين يتمكنون من السياحة حول العالم ، يشاهدون ويتعلمون وينفقون الكثير . لكن هؤلاء إستثناء من الشباب العربي ، ونحن نتحدث عن "القاعدة" غير المسافرين ، فثمة ألوف القاعدين . ألوف السواعد مسترخية ومعطلة ، طاقات هائلة كامنة وساكنة مدفونة في الشوارع والمنازل !

وللدقة فأن المشكلة ليست في فراغ الشباب فقط ولا في التفكير لمستقبل الشباب وحدهم ، لكنها في فراغ السياحة العربية ، على ما تحفل به من ضجيج ، وفي التفكير لمستقبل الأمة العربية على ما يحيط به من أخطار محدقة تلوح نذرها في الأفق الآن .

هي محنة أمة قبل أن تكون مشكلة شباب تائه ، حيرته سافرة خلال عطلة الصيف ، ومقنعة على مدار العام !

ومع ذلك نقول : أنقذوا الشباب العربي . أنقذوا عقله وجسده وروحه .
لأن هذا هو الطريق لإنقاذ المستقبل العربي !
(مجلة العربي : ص ٣ العدد ٢٣٦ يوليو (تموز) ١٩٧٨)

On the grammatical level, the text sets the scene for the reader by an adverbial clause of time (عندما يحل الصيف وتبدأ العطلات). The writer employs interrogative, imperative, and negative sentences (ماذا يفعلون لثلاثة أنقذوا الشباب) ,(ماذا يفعل الشباب طوال أشهر الصيف ؟) ,(أو أربعة أشهر قادمة ؟ ذلك) ,(السؤال لا يشغل الكثير من الذين . .) ,(أنقذوا عقله وجسده وروحه) ,(العربي لا يؤجل المشكلة) and (إن المشكلة ليست في فراغ الشباب فقط). The present tense is used throughout as in (يفكرون ، يخططون ، يعاني ، يأخذ ، يحل). The text is dominated by basic verbal sentences while derived sentences are used very rarely as in (السؤال لا يشغل الكثيرين). Nominal sentences without a verb are also used twice as in (ألوف السواعد مسترخية . .) ,(هي محنة أمة . .). We can also notice the use of the first person plural pronoun as in (نقول ، نحن نتحدث), the dominance of transitive verbs although the text starts off with intransitive ones (يحل , تبدأ) ,(يتعلم , يشاهد , يفكر , يخطط). We also find the dominance of two prepositions (في , من).

On the lexical level, it is a text highly charged with emotive clauses and expressions like (الشباب) ,(أخطار محدقة تلوح نذرها في الأفق رؤية) ,(حيرته سافرة) and (إنقاذ) ,(محنة) ,(أخطار) ,(مدفون) ,(التائه والحائر) ,(المستقبل جسده وروحه). The use of these emotive expressions reflect the writer's personal beliefs and his suggestions to solve a social problem. Comparative expressions are also used as in (قلة) and (نحن نتحدث عن "القاعدة" غير المسافرين). Descriptive words are recurrently used like (مقنَّع ، سافر ، محدق ، مدفون ، ساكن ، كامن ، هائل ، معطَّل ، مسترخي ، حائر ، تائه) to add an emphatic effect to the text. The use of inanimate abstract nouns is also found (مستقبل ، مشكلة ، الحاح ، أخطار ، حيرة ، فراغ).

On the cohesion level, the text employs adversative conjunctions like (لكن ، أنما), causal conjunction (لأن) and starts off with a temporal conjunction (عندما). Lexical cohesion is achieved through the use of synonyms like (حائر = تائه) ,(مسترخي = معطَّل) ,(ساكن = كامن) ,(مشكلة = أخطار) ,(محنة) and through collocation like (طاقات هائلة كامنة وساكنة) ,(محدقة). Antonyms are also used as in (مقنَّعة = سافرة). The text uses formal words and is free from calques and loan words. Reiteration of lexical expressions is employed effectively to highlight the problem (عربي ، المستقبل ، الصيف ، شارع ، أشهر ، ألوف ، الشباب). Verbal substitution is also used where the pronoun (هي) substitutes the verbal sentence (عندما يحل الصيف وتبدأ العطلات يأخذ الفراغ يعاني منه الشباب العربي صبغة "رسمية" ويمتلئ الشارع لألوف الألوف الذي من الشباب والحائر) and the pronoun (هذا) substitutes the imperative sentences (أنقذوا الشباب العربي . أنقذوا عقله وجسده وروحه). The lexical item (هي) is also employed as an exophoric reference. Extended, personal, and anaphoric reference are also used (هؤلاء ، هو ، ـه ، ها).

On the textual level, the text is a through-argumentation in which the writer presents a proposition highlighting a social problem of the youths during the summer holidays, that it is a waste of their potentials, and that this should be solved in the interest of the youths and the future of the Arab nation.

The major rhetorical hallmarks of the text are the use of hyperbole as in (أخطار محدقة ، ألوف السواعد ، ألوف الألوف), assonance as in (يشاهدون , ينفقون , يتعلمون), and irony (sarcasm) as in (سواعد مسترخية ومعطلة , طاقات . . مدفونة في الشوارع والمنازل), rhetorical questions as in (ماذا يفعلون لثلاثة أو أربعة أشهر قادمة), zeugma as in (يمتلىء الشارع) represented by the word (يمتلىء), and alliteration as in (أو أربعة أشهر).

Practical Exercises

تطبيقات

1. Provide a thorough stylistic analysis of the following texts using the grammatical, lexical, cohesive, textual, and rhetorical checklist:

١. توفى محمود تيمور يوم ٢٥ أغسطس ١٩٧٣ عن تسعة وسبعين عاماً . كان رائداً من رواد القصة المصرية وعلماً من أعلام الأدب العربي المعاصر . فلقد أعطى تيمور للأدب خالص حبه ووجدانه ، ووهب للقصة بالذات كل جهوده وصحته وقراءاته وكتاباته ، فأسهم منذ مطلع نهضتنا الأدبية حتى الآن بكتابة القصة في كافة صورها ، قصيرة أو طويلة أو ممثلة . وتيمور رائد بلا شك ، رائد كبير له تلاميذ ومريدون ، ويكفيه فخراً أنه من أوائل واضعي الأساس للقصة العربية . . ولا غرو أن يكون تيمور أديباً متميزاً ورائداً أعترف به الكافة ، فلقد نشأ في بيئة كلها أدب وأدباء ، فوالده المرحوم أحمد تيمور باشا كان عالماً جليلاً وباحثاً أصيلاً . . وأخوه محمد تيمور كان قد سافر الى باريس ليُحصِّل العلم ففتنه المسرح هناك وفتنته الحياة الأدبية وفتنته المسرحية والقصة القصيرة . . فلما عاد الى وطنه نادى بما أعجبه وأوضح ما زاد به كلفاً . . وبث محمد تيمور في أخيه محمود تيمور هذه الروح الجديدة . . ونشط محمود لعمله وخطا على الدرب في تؤدة وحذر ونفض عن كتفه اليأس ، وأقصى شبح الإخفاق ، معولاً على نفسه . ولم يكتف تيمور بأن يكون أديباً قصصياً ومسرحياً فحسب وإنما هو كاتب رحلات من الطراز الأول . . ولقد ساعدته أسفاره المتعددة على أن يكتب عنها بقلم الأديب الساحر وأن يتناولها بنظرة الأدب المتعمق . . والكاتب الفنان حين يرحل يحمل معه روحه ونفسه وقلمه فهو ينقل مشاعره على الورق حتى ليُخيِّلُ اليك وأنت تقرأه أنك ماض معه مطوفاً في البلاد والأنحاء .

(مجلة العربي : عدد ١٨٣ فبراير (شباط) ١٩٧٤ ص . ٤٠-٤٣)

٢. إنطلاقاً من أهداف مركز دراسات الخليج العربي في دراسة كل ما يتعلق بشؤون الخليج العربي ومن كافة النواحي الإجتماعية والسياسية والأدبية وعقد المؤتمرات العلمية ، إعتاد المركز عقد ندوات علمية يُدعى اليها باحثون متخصصون من المهتمين بشؤون الخليج العربي . وكان ذلك في آذار ١٩٧٥ وقد حضر تلك الندوة مختصون وباحثون من مختلف الأقطار العربية والأجنبية . وفي هذا العام ١٩٧٧ عقد مركز دراسات الخليج العربي ندوته العلمية العالمية الثانية وكان الهدف منها إلقاء الضوء على النتاج الفكري والثقافي لمنطقة الخليج العربي . حضر الندوة أكثر من مائة وخمسين شخصية علمية بين باحث متخصص وأستاذ جامعي من داخل القطر العراقي ومن أقطار الخليج العربي وبقية الأقطار العربية الأخرى ومن أوربا وأمريكا واليابان . واشتملت الندوة

على ست جلسات عمل أُلقيت فيها خلاصات لبحوث مختارة تقع ضمن الهدف العام للندوة . وفي الجلسة الختامية ألقى ألسيد رئيس الجلسة ألبيان ألختامي والتوصيات التي أقرها المؤتمرون وهي :

١. يؤكد المؤتمرون أن الخليج العربي تأريخياً وثقافياً جزء لا يتجزء من الوطن العربي الكبير ، وأن اللغة العربية ، وهي أداة التخاطب المشتركة ومن أهم عوامل الوحدة التي تربط الأقطار العربية تتعرض لخطر نتيجة إنتشار العجمة .

٢. الدعوة الى تأسيس منظمات للأدباء الخليجيين .

٣. يدعوا المؤتمرون الى ضرورة دراسة تراث هذه المنطقة .

٤. ترجمة ونشر الكتب والدراسات الخاصة بمنطقة الخليج العربي .

٥. الدعوة الى أن تكون مثل هذه الندوات دورية .

(مجلة الخليج العربي : العدد الثامن ١٩٧٧ ص ١٢١-١٢٣)

٣. حافظي على صحتك طوال فترة الحمل . إحرصي على زيارة الطبيب في فترات منتظمة أثناء الحمل . راعي أن تكون ملابسك واسعة ومريحة ونظيفة . لا تقومي بأعمال شاقة . لا تسافري سفراً طويلاً خاصة في الشهور الاولى من الحمل . إحرصي على نظافة جسمك بالإستحمام مرة في اليوم . وفري لنفسك الهدوء والسعادة . لا تُعرضي نفسك للانفعالات . لاحظي أن يحتوي طعامك على كل ما يحتاجه جسمك من العناصر الغذائية المتنوعة والكاملة . تناولي كميات كبيرة من السوائل . إحذري من تناول كميات كبيرة من الطعام حتى لا يزداد وزنك زيادة مفرطة . إبتعدي عن تناول الادوية إلاّ للضرورة وبعد إستشارة الطبيب .

(الثقافة العامة / للصف الاول / سلطنة عُمان - وزارة التربية : ١٩٩١ ص ٨٧)

Bibliography

Abdul-Raof, H. (1997). "al-muhaddath 'anhu fi thaw' al-nathariyyat al-lughawiyyah al-mu'asirah". In *al-Majallah al-Arabiyyah lil-Dirasat al-Lughawiyyah*. Vol. 9, No. 15; pp.35-46.

___ (1998). *Subject, Theme, and Agent in Modern Standard Arabic*. Surrey: Curzon.

Brook, G. L. (1979). *Varieties of English*. London: Macmillan.

Bushrui, S. B. (1970). *An Introduction to Khalil Gibran*. Beirut: Dar El-Mashreq.

Cuddon, J. A. (1977). *A Dictionary of Literary Terms*. London: Andre Deutsch.

Freeborn, D. (1996). *Style: Text Analysis and Linguistic Criticism*. London: Macmillan.

Halliday, M. A. K. and Hasan, R. (1976). *Cohesion in English*. London: Longman.

Kabbani, N. (1993). *Arabian Love Poems*. London: Lynne Rienner.

Leech, G. N. and Short, M. H. (1981). *Style in Fiction. A Linguistic Introduction to English Fictional Prose*. London: Longman.

Short, M. (1996). *Exploring the Language of Poems, Plays and Prose*. London: Longman.

Sulaiman, K. A. (1984). *Palestine and Modern Poetry*. London: Zed Books Ltd.

Wales, K. (1989). *A Dictionary of Stylistics*. London: Longman.

Widdowson, H. G. (1975). *Stylistics and the Teaching of Literature*. London: Longman.

Wright, L. and Hope, J. (1996). *Stylistics: A Practical Coursebook*. London: Routledge.

Index